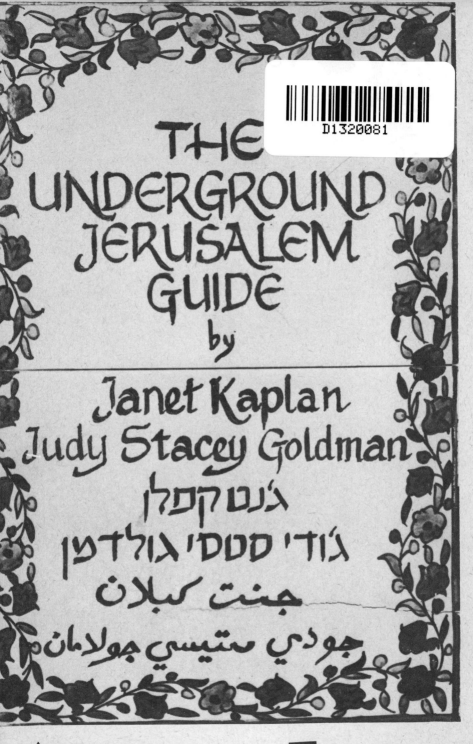

THE UNDERGROUND JERUSALEM GUIDE

by

Janet Kaplan
Judy Stacey Goldman

ג'נט קפלן
ג'ודי סטסי גולדמן

جنت كبلان
جودي ستيسي جولدمان

KETER BOOKS

STEIMATZKY

Cover:
Hand-crafted tile by Setrak N. Balarian
Photographed by:
Zev Radovan
Door courtesy of:
Tova Mizrachi
Book Art and Design:
Nomi Morag
Decorative Designs:
Marie Balarian
Photos:
Janet Kaplan
Pages 53, 69 by Alexandra Dor-Ner

First Printing, November 1976
Second Printing, January 1977

Cat. No. 262177

Keter Publishing House, Jerusalem Ltd.
Givat Shaul, Jerusalem, Israel

PRINTED IN ISRAEL

JERUSALEM LOVE

To JS, the Generator;
to Ulysses (from Molly)
for quintessential albeit
sporadic magifications;
to Marjorie of Malibu;
to the Big B for solar
relief during the snows
of yesteryear; to Aaron
the Arieh (Jewish Guru);
to Boje Him Self; to
FF, the Paradigm of
Panache; to Peter the
Great for getting her
there and back way
beyond the haul of duty;
to our English
Mayorella; to Easy
Rider; to the Two
Cockatoos of Katamon;
to Paul, Rafi, and
Micha (suns all).

A FABLE OF CONTENTS

Jerusalem Day & Night

It is dusk in Jerusalem, the City of Mankind,
the City of Peace, Jerusalem the Eternal,
the Holy. The sun sets lovingly once more on
her aged stones, lighting them with pink and
bronze, copper, dun and gold. Heaven holds a
place for our sacred city.

The gold that is Jerusalem glows with a beauty
and a glory of its own. Her light is warmth and
a blessing to all who live and love within the
comfort of her grace and dignity.

Church bells and carillons ring through the soft
air of David's city. The *muezzin* sings his song
of summons as barefoot Moslems fall to their
knees in reverence, foreheads touching the
silken prayer rugs on the floor of the Mosque.
Richly robed Christian priests lead their
faithful in ceremonial pomp. At ancient
shrines, pilgrims pray to the glory of the
Prince of Peace. Rabbis and their pupils,
wrapped in black-striped shawls, chant the
timeless Hebrew prayers in atonal unison; and
for the billionth time the ancient stones of the
Western Wall absorb their whispered words of
wish and gratitude.

8

As the last of day's light withdraws from the holy sites, a small flock of sheep bumbles homeward over the rocky fields below Mount Zion.

The opaque gold light finally succumbs to gentle dark, and stars settle in close above our domes, minarets and steeples. A satisfying peace pervades.

It is real: the ineffable quality of holiness that fills the night air of Jerusalem with a suspenseful yearning and the hint of an imminent response.

Then, up comes the dawn

MORNING BECOMES ELECTRIC
and our happy holy city turns on:

With the bang of the first-opened shutter and the clang of unlocking gates, everyday Jerusalem swings into making her daily bread : the profits of prophets become the business of life. It's the clanging of cash registers, the banging of beads, hawking, hondelling and the hooting of horns.

Ours is a nonstop scene seven days a week. Each of the three great religions celebrates its own holy day : on Fridays the Moslems are doing it, on Saturdays the Jews, and Sundays the Christians. Everybody's doing it one day or another, but meanwhile, and in between, everybody else is not. P.S. : on Saturdays the circus shifts to the Old City, a potential retail-religious Disneyland. Daytime Jerusalem is a fast tango in God's little acres.

Jerusalem is also the original Scene of the Total Costume. You'll see them all : dudes and dowdies festooned in full folk array, homespun habits, hooded monk frocks, long black embroidered Bedouins, micro-minis, saris, sandals and sneakers. A turban here, a fez there, yarmulkes, babushkas, facial tattoos. Patched jeans and pantaloons and priests in pigtail. Tourist Guccis among other bags of straw and string. Wigs, shades, stars, and scimitars—all in living color.

It's the Home of the Felafel Ball.
Land for the Brave.
The whole earth spectrum—secular to
spiritual—vibrates in neo-dayglow. Animals!
Real and live! Eleemosynaries in action!
It's sack cloth and asses in the Phantom Jet
Age of Aquarius.

Traffic snarls to a
stop while a piled-
up donkey trundles
across the street....
You can rent a
helicopter to buzz
around in the blue,
but in town you ride
the behemoth buses,
loaded with wild-
type people carrying
anything: toilet
seats, live chickens,
kerosene cans, sabra
fruits (with prickles)
and sometimes even
each other. And
while computers calculate the fortunes of
business, a village vendor weighs your cluster
of grapes with stones on a scale made of a stick,
string, and 2 tin plates. Past, present, and future
are all one tense in Jerusalem—ingathered
and outgoing.

One thinks of Jerusalem as a big city:
because it is a world capital, because it is
historically heavy and the spiritual center of
three major religions and always making media
hotnews. But it is not. It's really smalltown—a
mountain village in fact and feeling. Fun and
unique, however, is its compleat collection of
human life in all its styles.
We've got eclectic ethnics. An allsorts array of
locals: weird and wonderful, plain and fancy,
sexy and solemn. Some beyond the fringe,
beyond the pale, the blue horizon; and some
certainly beyond belief. Jerusalem is a tiny
textured world of curious crowdy colors. A
macromixed bag, our town.

All the mystery and charm and seductiveness of
Jerusalem at night reveals itself in the bright
light of day only behind the upfront downtown
scene. So come with us

CIRCUMFORANEOUS⋆

(⋆from Latin: *circum*: around; *forum*:
marketplace; literally: wandering about the
marketplace)
It's a whole different trip. Riding as we do out
of the West, we are used to prepackaged
everything, polyethylene wrapped,
hermetically sealed, factory inspected and
off-the-rack. But here we trade convenience for
charm (or a Mediterranean facsimile thereof).

Come with us out of the center city, off the well-pounded pavements. Traipse off the track. Backalley it : up the stairs, under the arch, around the bend, into the pits, the attics, the caves. To be believed, this scene must be seen and felt and tasted.

Straights can make the Jerusalem trip with any old guide or book. Our shaggydog salleys, however, make it through the underground. We avoid the tracks so well trodden over the ages by crusaders of all ilk: Romans, Turks, UJAviators and Holy Spiriters.

Jerusalem is a Chinese box of secret surprises. Fortressed, crenellated and courtyarded. The farther in you get, the more you walk and wait and watch, the better your chances for connecting with the goodguys, honest hospitality and the pleasure of seeing whole processes : raw materials being transformed into treasures. It is here that you will also meet the ingroupers, the invisibles, the cave dwellers, cliff hangers, the crafties, the charmers, aesthetes and effetes who have come from corners of the world you never knew existed.

In here, on the inside, it all hangs out along with the laundries of life. Ethnic everything in pocket neighborhoods. It's not homogenized. Jerusalem is a mad marvel of a mosaic. And it is endless, our tiny town.

Ours is not a bargain-hunter's book, nor a critical, complete survey of available goods and services. Ours is a lover's guide; and whether your love is people, art, photography or crafts, you are bound to discover a special someone or something that pops up only for you in the patchwork orange of daytime Jerusalem.

At the time of interview, all underground persons were alive, all places were real and all prices were true. But due to the vagaries of fate, inflation, weather, etcetera, you may not find each as is writ. (As in phone numbers: please call Information at 14 if the number you are calling is unreachable).
Ahem. Should you therefore follow the verse of our chapters and discover that the underground shifts and wiggles and does not always rhyme with reality, do not despair: another serendipity will no doubt surface in its stead.

Loominary

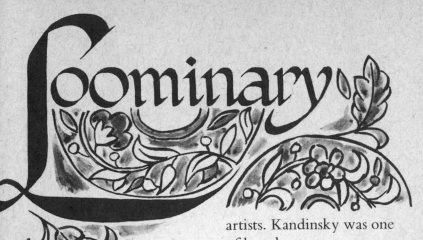

Ruth Kaiser weaves wondrous wall hangings—big, beautiful visions of Jerusalem. Without a pre-planned design, she works up the mountains, valleys, forests and deserts that surround our city in all their dramatic texture and density.

Her lovely home is also a lofty studio: 2 enormous wooden looms, tons of wool (some homespun, some self-dyed) and an endless view of the Ein Kerem forested valley. Mrs. Kaiser is a graduate of the Bauhaus, where she trained together with some of today's most celebrated artists. Kandinsky was one of her classmates.

Her wall hangings are deep, heavy, luxurious and extraordinary works of art—no two are alike—sized for palaces and fit for kings. Diffident about "making sales," Mrs. K. has begun to accept a limited number of special orders. Whatever the price, they are worth it. She is a hospitable and lovely lady, and the hills of Jerusalem are honored by her talent.

Ruth Kaiser
Address: ask her
Kiryat Hayovel, Jerusalem West
Phone: 413168, early mornings, for appointment
Dialogue in: English, Hebrew, German

Said* Saddle

(*pronounced: Sigh-eed)
Bottom blue from riding horseback? Let Said Joudeh make you a real leather saddle, English or Western style. For aesthetic equestrians, he also sells bridles, buckles, belts and accessories, including a delicately decorative white braid of a horsedressing (a *rassia*) handwoven by the Bedouin.

Said comes from a Jerusalem family whose honor it was to be the keepers of the keys to the Church of the Holy Sepulchre. If your horse sense is none, have a look at his sandals, belts and pouches.

Said Joudeh
32 Akabat Kahan el-Akbat Street
(Halfway down Christian Quarter Street, left up the alley steps, and left side in)
Old City
No Phone
Hours: 8–7; closed Sunday
Dialogue in: English Arabic, Hebrew

The Jerusalem Connection

A marriage broker. Our pre-interview expectations: an old bearded man holding a plumed pen over a cracked leather ledger on a high oak desk who wants your life savings to fix you up with his nephew/niece. Wrong! Michael (he was an angel, remember?) is 32, kindly, cute and sincere. He's from Russia with love on his mind. As a student at the Hebrew University, he saw that the social situation in Jerusalem leaves a drop to be desired, especially if one's status is single. The City of Peace can oft be a ho-hummer, so Michael started a social club, getting it together on weekends, plus a meet-each-other service as well. Now he's finished his studies (Hebrew language and psychology) and is a fulltime broker. He even married a client!

Michael takes your basic non-depth details and several hundred Israeli pounds, which registers and connects you for one year. Most of the work is done by phone. He has an equal number of men and women registered. His youngest client was 18 and the oldest, 60—she's married now. Credential: we liked him and his style of "disturbing" the peace.

Reut ("Friendship")
13 Elazar Hamodai, Apt. 7
German Colony, Jerusalem West
Phone: 60845, anytime, keep trying
Dialogue in: Russian, Hebrew, English, Polish, Yiddish

19

 DEEP TOTE

Baskets of every shape, depth, weave and width— flat, fat, tall, wide and weird—all wickered by the Bedouin deep down in the Sinai Desert. They are available everywhere in the Old City. But our vote for top totery goes to Maged Sueiti.

Down David Street and go, go, go past the cave of the vegetable market on the left and the raw hanging meat on the right. Take a right past the meat at Suk el-Hussor Street. There'll be a wicker place on the left and again on the right but keep on straight ahead to Sueiti's (facing you). He's a good guy, and his selection of straw also includes furniture. Indigenous imperatives are the brown twiggies woven from tiny olive-tree branches, arty and useful. He sometimes also has heavy round woven-straw trays that look like super soup bowls (called *junehs*), which are a great bargain. More bread, but well worth it, are his baskets with lids: fine for laundry or toys, but especially appealing to the latent snake charmers among us.

Maged Sueiti
40 Suk el-Hussor
Old City
Home phone: 284324
Hours: 9–5 or so; closed Friday
Dialogue in: Any/all Arabic dialects plus English and Hebrew

Tally of the dolls

Need a doll for your house? One to be scene and not heard, with limber limbs and a secret personality? Tala creates ceramic metaphors of her friends and relatives, doll people of varying size (some are 2 feet tall) and

mien. You'll love her grandmother—she's riding a bike! Tiny Tala was born on a kibbutz and now teaches pottery at the Israel Museum. She's about half as high as her bright yellow garden gate and whirls the wheel in her old stone home. The workshop's in the basement and the kiln's in the garden shed. Inside, the stairway displays her cloud-colored ceramics: pots, sculptures and boxes, some of which hint and some of which reveal what's inside. Plus her very special mini mannequins.

Tala Ziv
1 Ehud Street
Bak'a, Jerusalem West
(Take Derech Bethlehem,
coming from town, turn
right onto Shimshon Street
across from No. 25. Right
again across from a red door
and shutters, and first left on
to the yellow garden gate)
Phone: 30714, for
appointment
Dialogue in: Hebrew and
British

Our seer, Greer, can read the future in your palm, the message in your melted candle, Turkish coffee sediment, playing cards—and soon to come: tarots! She is a fabulous find—charming, chatty, ebullient and warm-hearted. Her favorite and most serious concern is in-depth analytic studies made from palm prints, so complex that readings can take 4 to 6 weeks to complete.

Fate Accompli

To bring or mail her your palm prints, do like this: using mimeograph or printer's ink (removable with turpentine), print your palm, in a natural position, on soft white paper. Press down so you get all the tiny lines from

the wrist to finger tips (relax, then press). The print should look like a

reverse x-ray, and she needs 4 of each hand. Every bump (and grind), line and hollow counts. The palm patterns of the hand with which you write will reveal your destiny; the other hand reveals character.

Greer is Australian born and began by reading coffee sediment swirls during a visit to Cairo. Her gift for seeing beyond has developed over the years and has fully bloomed

in the mystical air of
Jerusalem.
Candle-wax readings are
another number,
Rorschach-type
interpretations. Ask her,
she'll tell all.
Good news: you don't
have to blow your fortune
to fly here and hear it. Just
send Greer $30 by
registered air mail (she's
honest, but this is your
proof), cool it for about a
month or so, and she will
mail you back a typed
analysis.

Greer Cashman
3 Smolenskin Street
Rehavia, Jerusalem West
Phone: 37191, for
appointment
Dialogue in: English,
Hebrew, Yiddish, German,
nonfluent Polish and Russian
if that'll help

Our culinary lesson for today is entitled: "Technological Treats from Terra Sancta, or, The Esoteric Art of Eshtanur" (flatter-than-*pita* Iraqi bread).

Do it as they do at Abib's: stand in front of a huge, coal-burning, white-hot oven (must be handmade). With the left hand, pick up a dough-ball from a wooden bin containing 2000 others. Hold *eshtanur* pillow in your right hand (pillow must be covered in striped satin) and adroitly throw the dough-ball from your left hand onto the pillow. Carefully smear dough onto the pillow to form a flat circle. With right arm outstretched, plaster the dough-side of the pillow to the inner wall of the oven. Watch out for burning coals below. Remove pillow—and hand. When the *eshtanur* is ready, it falls off the inner oven wall. Coolly accept applause from audience while stacking.

THE PILLOW CASE

There are only two places in Jerusalem where this incredible Iraqi bread-making process can be viewed and the bread bought hot off the oven wall:

Bakery Abib
60 Ussishkin Street
Jerusalem West
Hours: 7–4; Friday till
3:30; closed Saturday
Dialogue in: Hebrew, Arabic

Shuk Iraqi
Mahane Yehuda Market (off
Mahane Yehuda Street, off
Jaffa Road) Jerusalem West
(After turning off Mahane
Yehuda Street, keep left, pass
Abu Shaul's Restaurant,
watch for a burlap awning and
take a sharp left into a dark pit)
Hours: Probably as sbove
Dialogue in: Ditto

Leather Bound

Well, tan my hide if that dude in the long white dress ain't wearin' a hand-hewn leather belt with a real Sears Roebuck buckle. Can't imagine how he came by that old Texas type goodie here in the Holyland. "Say, mistah, where'd you all pick up that thar belt you got wrapped around your robe? Yea, the one holding up your sabre. . . . You say Allah gave it to you? Yawh. What spread does he come from? Ah mean, where can I find 'im?"

If you get your leather from Above, you don't need our help; but if not, there's a man in town who makes all kinds of great, villagey, tough stuff. Joe is an American anthropologist who works at the Rockefeller Museum by day. By night he creates chunky leather kit bags, pocketbooks, wide watch bands, belts with super buckles and other such specialties. All in fine taste and true talent. Uniquely his are Jesus- or Massada-style custom-made sandals (depending on your sole orientation).

Plans are already afoot for getting into gourds, and he has already planted the seeds. If they grow, Joe will dry, stain and wax them into bold, natural bowls.

He himself is a soft-spoken, creative guy, and Easy Rider handsome.

Joe Zias
8 Rehov Asa (under an arch
of greens) Greek Colony,
Jerusalem West
Telephone: 63012, for
appointment
Dialogue in: English and
Hebrew

M·U·S·H

The Israeli Breakfast of Champions—*hummus* in Hebrew—a foodpaste of ground chick-peas plus a goodly amount of garlic and lemon juice and a toss of fresh parsley. Instant energy and cheap; the local gourmand's monomania. Don't try this delicacy in any of the 2 million street stands. Eat it only at the best of places, Abu Shukri's, a wall-hole in the Old City, impeccably furnished in Mideast Woolworth Renaissance.

Those with iron-clad stomachs, the knights-errant among us, will take it on the chin, that is: sitting down. Hummus is served in a pool on a plate and you scoop it up with pieces of *pita* (Mideast flat bread). Kultur Kings eat it with a pouring of olive oil and side orders of devil-hot peppers, sour pickles and raw onion quarters (served skin and all). Sound good? Two toppings available: *fool* (cooked beans) or hot whole chick-peas—request your favorite.

It's the perfect start to a day of catacombing the Old City. Or bring your own container to have filled and take out. (An Abu Bonus: golden olive oil for sale; buy the bottle at a good price).

Abu Shukri
9 Aquabat el-Khanka Street
Old City (From Jaffa Gate
follow instructions to "Razz
Tattoo" 'page 90' but
continue down the street.
Abu's is on the left)
No phone
Hours: Dawn–7 P.M.;
closed Sunday
Dialogue in: Arabic,
Hebrew, easy English

27

Bestow a blessing on your home or synagogue. A paper-cut *mizrach*. Made in Jerusalem.

Paper cutting is an old Jewish folk craft, popular in the 19th century in Eastern Europe, lost for many, many years and now revived through Yehudit Shadur's talent and love for tradition.

their dreams, while Mrs. Shadur draws on her personal experience and perceptions of our holy city. One we especially liked was dark green, barely touching a beige background, highlighted by gold.

The Israel Museum acquired one of her *mizrachs* for its ethnic

Mrs. Shadur's first paper-cut *mizrach* (the word means east) was done to decorate the *sukkah*-booth at Kibbutz Sde Boker. David Ben-Gurion told her it was a most touching reminder of his childhood in Poland.

Mizrachs are placed on eastern walls, to direct prayers toward Jerusalem. They used to be done by men who never lived here and only saw Jerusalem in

collection—that's how great her work is. Choose from her selection or talk to her about a special order.

Yehudit Shadur
11 Alkalai Street, Entrance B (through the bushes)
Talbieh, Jerusalem West
Phone: 35198, evenings or before 8 a.m.
Dialogue in: Hebrew, English

Not just any son of a gun can buy a piece in Jerusalem. You have to get a permit from the Ministry of the Interior; and if game is your bag, you must get a license from the Department of Agriculture.

The House of Weaponry has been as is for over 50 years, originally opened by Mr. Ben Yehuda, who made it to Palestine on camelback in 1921 from Russia, via Bukhara, Afghanistan and India.

This house is thus firmly established as the major importers of guns and rifles from all over the world. Only the real thing: famous brands and live ammo. For constructive purposes only: they have an extensive supply of explosives, all accessories plus dynamite red flags.

Sporty Haim Shoshani now manages the bullets business. Practice makes perfect, so they say, but where? He says you can

some like it shot...

shoot in good sporting style at the I-say-Old-Man Allenby Barracks or at the Schneller Army Compound range. Check with duty officers first.

Beit Haneshek Hayerushalmi 9 King David Street (P.O.B. 120) Jerusalem West Phone: 225500 or 223773 Hours: 8–1 and 3:30–6; Friday till 1 ; closed Saturday Dialogue in: Hebrew and English

some like it hot...

... or cold, or icy, or even frozen hot—in the classiest café in town.

Fabulous Francine Friedman has done it again. She is our Lady of the Laurels—not that she rests on them. Having masterminded the renovation of the old-new home of Maskit, she's already into something new, yes, under the sun. Through the tint of her C. Diors, Ms. Friedman oversees an outré outback café to pamper Maskit customers.

Re. your thirst: they serve Mocha Coolers, fresh fruit drinks, U.S.A.-style icy coffee and tea, and would-you-believe Chocolate Egg Creams, plus other specials to quaff or quench it.

Re. your hunger: personally commissioned home-baked goodies to abate it.

Re. your waistline and pocketbook: forget it in this garden of earthly delights.

The Café at Beit Maskit
12 Harav Kook (entrance
only through the store)
Downtown Jerusalem West
Hours: 9–6
Phone: 227941
Dialogue in: Hebrew, Arabic,
Turkish, French, English,
German, Yiddish, Spanish,
Swedish, Danish, or as per
available staff

bookmaking

We'll swear to it on a Bible: Therese Mahler and Sidney Miroz are the answer to a bibliophile's prayer.

A French piano teacher and an Egyptian graphic artist team up to turn out handmade blank-page books from their beginnings—on an antique French press. Therese is the expert binder and restorer of priceless antique books as well. Sidney silk-screens handsome greeting cards (like "Happy New Year" in Rashi script), each card a gift in itself, limited and numbered. More graphically, we fainted over his facsimile of an 18th century *megillah* on pure parchment, a *haggadah* on hand-cut paper, and a triptych of the Sabbath prayer on wood and suede.

Cover to cover and page by page, theirs must be the most beautiful bindings under the sun. Like: bold red leather with gold studs; parchment decorated with a strip of Bedouin embroidery; semi-precious stones caught in a sterling-silver web on black leather—each more gorgeous than the other. They are fit for kings and presidents, princesses and museums. Also great for honored guests, moving memories, cherished collections, poems or photographs.

Mahler & Meroz Studio
Diskin Street (opposite No. 7
of the Kiryat Wolfson
buildings) Nachlat Zadok,
Jerusalem West (Go to end
of Ramban Street and turn
right onto Diskin, a dirt road)
No Phone
Hours: 8–4: closed Saturday
Dialogue in: Hebrew, French,
Arabic, English

32

The chic of Araby

For lessons in Arabic, classic or colloquial, reading, writing, or talking, contact Omar, a graduate of the Hebrew University, teacher and author. A serious, sophisticated and brainy guy, he'll turn you in the right direction for private lessons or small specialized classes. Omar is something of a Sharif type—definitely an added attraction to learning Arabic (or any language). The little red schoolhouse has changed . . .

Omar Ottman
Beit Safafa (Near the Katamonim. Coming from town, turn left off Ben Zakkai at Yossi Ben Yoezer Street and left again into the village of Beit Safafa. Left again to the second house.)
Phone: 65670
Dialogue in: Arabic (including all kinds of fancy Bedouin dialects), Hebrew and English

FOOLS' SCHOOL

If the Hebrew University catalogue does not inspire you, may we present a dazzling alternative: a three-month Clown Course, with Gadi Roll. He is Our Town's best Bozo, he's 17 years old, and he's been studying and performing for 8 years, in Europe and the U.S. (Gadi's School gives short-term workshops too, for children and adults, which may be hired out by institutions, groups, schools and such). The Course includes unicycling, fire eating, theatrical improvisation, juggling and tap-dancing and you'll be able to show off your skills during the student street performances. You on a unicycle in Zion Square . . .

Gadi Roll
House 36, Area Daled
Ein Kerem
Phone: 415677
Dialogue in: Hebrew, English, Arabic, bits of French and Spanish

The Ice Blues

Yukhh. No air conditioning. No palmetto fan, and no Nubian slave to wave one. Air heavy with *khamsin* (dry desert air). Yesterday's dust storm left silt on your soul. The Middle East sun bubbles and boils. Drippy, slippy, dense desert heat. The shower is lukewarm, dacron droops, streaked hair straggles, home is a hothouse and the iceman never cometh in summertime Jerusalem. So we goeth to him. Here are two places where you can buy much more of a supply than you can collect from your neighbors:

The American Colony Hotel
Nablus Road (just past St. George's Compound)
Jerusalem East
Phone: 282421 (ask for Mrs. Jasper—and give her at least one day's notice)
Hours: Hotelish
Dialogue in: British best

Abu Sali
Hanevi'im Street
Jerusalem East (Straight out from the Damascus Gate, two pit stops after the Egged bus sign, to the right of Askar Paints)
No Phone
Hours: 6–6; Sunday 10 till high noon
Dialogue in: Arabic and easy Hebrew
N.B.: Here the ice comes in poles. IL 6 or so per 1-yard length weighing approximately 25 kilos or 50 pounds. Abu has been into ice for half a century. He has become something of an ice polecat, and cool.

a Glad Hatter

S. has spent 50 of them making hats: Chassidic velvets, *yeshivah*-boy black wide-brims, straws, felts, stovepipes, panamas and top hats.

Stop preening long enough to take a look at the backroom workshop: a mini-museum of old-world hatwork supplies. Mr. Singler is a gentle elderly man with a marvelous memory, and he is a fine craftsman.

You are looking so chic in your tails: bow tied, bib tucked and cummer bound. All set for dinner with the Pres and damned if you can find your top hat. Off you go to Singler's, where the 75-year-old Mr.

Singler Hat Store
59 Ussishkin Street
Jerusalem West
Phone: 231643
Hours: 9–1 and 3–6;
Friday 9–3; closed Saturday
Dialogue in: Polish, Hebrew,
German, Yiddish and a little
Arabic to top it off

A great escape from the strife of commercial life. Hide from your guide! Eschew Egged! Return to the earth, the soil, the land itself. Feel it, be touched, and love it together with the most idealistic Israelis of all: Haganat Hateva ("The Society for the Protection of Nature").

They sponsor priceless walking tours at NO cost. J-(as in Jerusalem) walk with trained guides and/or archaeologists: do the Western Wall Dig, a

town and all over our wonderful country too. Or become a member, even *in absentia*, to support the will of their good. Tours are conducted mostly in Hebrew, but there will always be someone along who speaks your language. Detailed itineraries are available through the two Government Tourist Offices and at Society headquarters.

land lovers

Botanical Walk, Bird Watch, Follow the Footsteps of the '48 Fighters, or Light Flares for the New Moon of *Iyar*.

Become a member to take advantage of other tours in

Haganat Hateva
13 Queen Helene Street
Russian Compound,
Jerusalem West
Phone: 222357
Hours: 9–noon

Service for Ate

Why did the chicken cross the Via Dolorosa? To get to the other side . . . where he could choose his very own Armenian hand-painted plate. There is no better way to dish it out than on this densely decorated pottery. Lovely to look at and a pleasure to use: dinner dishes, mugs, cream-and-sugar sets, hors d'oeuvres platters, ashtrays, bowls and bells to ring in the maid. Door and drawer knobs too.

The tiles are terrific. Some are cork-backed to use as trivets, others are framed for hanging and some are made to be fitted into table tops (like the four-tile "Tree of Life" design). Some say "Shalom"—we are all saying it. Jerusalem Pottery made all the street-sign tiles that decorously direct you inside the Old City. You'll see them on every corner, written in our three local languages: Hebrew, Arabic and English.

Good to know: the amiable Armenians are also amenable to your special-order idea.

Jerusalem Pottery
Stefan and Berge Karakashian
15 Via Dolorosa (near the
Sixth Station of the Cross)
Old City
No phone
Hours: 8–5:30; closed
Sunday
Dialogue in: Armenian,
Arabic, English, French,
Turkish, a little Hebrew too

The Stern Gang

It's the type of shop you could pass a million times. The windows display insecticides, aerosols, household hardware, tourist trinkets, and drugstore doodads. Not exactly enticing to undergrounders. The sign out front says "Herzl's Room." Big deal, you might think. But turns out it is. The Stern father, Yehuda, arrived in Palestine in 1870 and built the house, one of the first Jewish homes outside the Old City and certainly a first on Mamilla Street.

While Theodor Herzl was stomping for the Jewish state around 1898, he stayed here in the bosom of the Sterns (there being no room, as usual, at the inn, which was then all occupied by Wilhelm the Emperor of Germany & Entourage).

Today, the shop is a house is a shop and a minimuseum, brimful of historical mementos of Herzl and old Jerusalem at the turn of the century.

Although she may not have a Ph.D. in window dressing, Ruth Stern (a fascinating Simone Signoret type) does have one in criminology, and from Oxford. Plus there's brother Meir, engineer, photographer and raconteur, as well as sister two, Chana, a ballet dancer.

And do they have groove for sale: all kinds of antiques and jewelry which is super-sensational stuff that will grab the gypsy in your soul. Heavy, fancy, intricate, colorful, weird exotica, the real thing and fun fakeries. Ankle bangles, nose rings, bellydance belts, everything you could never imagine and from countries you maybe never knew existed, like Turkestan (now nowhere but formerly between Iran and Siberia), the Atlas Mountain area (North Africa, from Morocco to Tunisia) and good old Afghanistan. The shop itself, its view, the family, are all a special story: it's written in what we presume to be impeccable Hebrew in their brochure. They will explain in the Queen's English, if you are nice and not rushy.

Michael Stern
18 Mamilla Street (P.O.B.
631) Jerusalem West
Hours: 9–1 and 4–7;
Museum, 10–12; groups
should call for an
appointment
Phone: 226719
Dialogue in: Hebrew,
English

Software

Their work looks as they do—delicate, gentle and softly colored. In a notably serene setting, especially for mid-city, you walk down the worn stone steps and enter their well-tended flower-full garden. Inside, you can sometimes see a sister at work.

They also make tiles to order for bathroom or kitchen walls. (Pat Rainey of "Body Works" [see page 119] has some of their fish in her bathroom and soft pastel thistles in her kitchen.)

The homespun-blue-clad Sisters live on the premises, so speak softly and leave your big stick at home. A limited but lovely selection.

The Little Sisters of Jesus don't seek publicity, so we are whispering that they make decorative ceramic and enamel items such as vases, pots, ashtrays, crosses on leather strings and candlesticks for Hannukkah.

The Little Sisters of Jesus
18 Mamilla Road (near "Herzl's Room" not far from the Jaffa Gate)
Jerusalem West
Hours: General business ones; closed Sunday
Dialogue in: Impeccable Hebrew, French, a little English

a Silver Lining

Once you've copped yourself a pot, brass or copper, you may find its insides need re-tinning. So *schlep* over to Suq el-Lahhamin Street, behind the Church of the Redeemer in the Old City. On the corner of the street is a vegetable stall, next is a metal fixer, next a suede stitcher and next is a cave where a white-mustachioed gentleman is in with tin. Our inside job cost IL 12 for an eight-incher—obviously one of the last of the lead-hot bargains!

We could not understand if "Armeni" was his name or his origin. But he'll give you a stool so you can sit and watch while this tintype repairs over hot sparky coals.

Hours: Pot luck
Dialogue in: Arabic, Turkish, maybe Armenian

43

asseemoneem

Transliteration of Hebrew: telephone tokens. If you don't have one handy when you need it, you're outta luck with Ma Bell in Jerusalem. *Asseemoneem* look like iron bagels for midgets and are equally available. So stock up with a good supply in the Post Office first chance.

"BARKING"
Transliteration of Arabic: parking (there's no "p" sound in Arabic).
The most heinous of Israeli crimes is parking in a no-parking zone. By the way (pun), moving violations

are low priority here: you can pass on the right—

without signaling—up a blind hill, all at top speed, and no one will notice or care. But park in a no-parking zone and police appear as if out of the pavement.
The best bargain in Jerusalem (freebies excluded), and maybe in the world, is the parking lot at the bottom of Hillel Street, city center. Cost: pennies per hour. Park here even if your camel is a mile away and you have to walk . . .

"BOLICE"
How to get 'em: park in a no-parking zone.

Cooking Glass

Through the dark to see the glass we go. It's a big bad black square cave, and the glow comes from Mohammed's earthen oven. He and/or son sits in the doorway of said oven, blowing into the bright orange blast. Our heroes' hotlips produce a twisty assortment of pitchers, bowls, glasses, plates, winecups, charms, floats and vases in tough colors of turquoise, brown, green, blue. Nifty gifties. Extra! Extra! Read All About It . . . Mohammed's Action Electrifies Metal Chandelier! Near the entrance is another workshop, where they make great chandeliers. Mo will fit one out with home-blown glass cups to hold light bulbs or candles, depending on which light is best for romantic you.

Mohammed Raslan Kazza &
Family
Monumental Glass Factory
Old Ideal Technical Mfg.
Wadi Joz (right
behind Suleiman's, see "On
the Safe Side, page 67)
East of Jerusalem East
Phone: 282257
Hours: 8–5 all week
Dialogue in: Arabic,
Turkish, Hebrew

It is simply not done to do your thing in Jerusalem without a goodly supply of seeds and/or nuts in hand. Pack them in your sack or pile them in your pockets and then ask an Israeli to give you a Between the Teeth Lesson: How to Eat a Seed While Shedding the Shell While Talking.

Get Thee to a Nuttery

The best places to get your crunchies are where they roast them, and here are 2 places in the alley called Yanetz Street (between Ben Hillel and Jaffa). They both sell hot, fresh-roasted almonds, shelled sunflower seeds, chick-peas, pecans, filberts and pine nuts (in season). Apricot "leather" from Turkey too.

On the right (coming from Jaffa) is *Yosef Bahari's shop.* Too bad you missed the sign he just took down. It read: "This store is not shared or tied to any other—not in name or in work." You see, there once was a family named Bahari and two of their menfolk were in the nut business since 1958. In 1967, they drove each other nuts arguing, and so they split. Now Yosef is here with his shop and Eliahu has his own nuthouse across and up the alley. *Yosef works from 8 a.m.–10 p.m. without a break; Friday till 4; closed Saturday. He sells in Hebrew and Arabic.*

Eliahu Bahari does not have a sign in his shop, but he does have brown gingham formica decor. Good toasted roasteds. *Open 8 a.m.–9 p.m.; Friday till dusk; closed Saturday. Sales in Hebrew, Arabic, a little English.*

Here's what to do if your barefeet, Jesus sandals, sneakers or high-heeled cloppers are killing you after miles and hours of walking: save your soles at Dr. Scholl's.

Often unavailable as a street-side service in the States and/or hard to find and/or expensive, here's an effete service available in Jerusalem, above board, easy to find and a bargain to boot.

Although the interior is faintly reminiscent of a medieval torture chamber, don't be put off. You'll find all manner of remedy for problems of feckless feet. And a gentle lady will carve off your calluses with surprising delicacy while you sit perched in your pedestal chair.

Dr. Scholl's
50 Jaffa Road
Jerusalem West
Phone: 225016; appointments
a must.
Hours: 8:30–1 and 3:30–7;
closed Tuesday and
Friday afternoons
and Saturdays
Dialogue in: Hebrew, various
European, some English

FOOTNOTES

KIDNIGHT COWBOY

Sometimes your own kids can be too much, but on their birthdays you have them and all their little kamikaze friends too. To calm them down and quiet the scene, how about movies at home.

Abu and Zwili will rent you real flicks, plus the projector. Subjects are suitable for little minds: Charlie Chaplin, Laurel & Hardy, Dastardly & Muttley, cartoons and cowboys. They are silent (like the kids could be, heh heh), they're in living black and white, 8 mm. You must put down a deposit of IL 500 (Abu will take a check)—but for our children nothing is too much.

Each film is IL 5 and the projector goes for IL 40. But if you're not up to projecting, Abu can sometimes send someone to do it for you.

Wholesale photo supplies and other equipment rentals too.

Photo Yehezkel
47 Jaffa Road
Downtown Jerusalem West
(Near the King George and Jaffa intersection, look for the sign that says "Yehezkel" on the alley entrance)
Phone: 225590
Hours: 8:30–1:30 and 4–7; Friday till 2:30; closed Saturday
Dialogue in: Hebrew, English, Arabic, one brother speaks French

48

KARMA SUTURE

Studio 51 is Annette Fein's hip home and arts studio. She's multi-talented, but her singular specialty is three-dimensional embroidered graphics. She begins them as paintings and then transforms the design into triumphal textured tapestries. Wools in all warm colors, wondrous and wild. Each wall hanging is individually mounted and ready to frame. Newest are her tiny dense numbers. Like sunbursts.
Each is a Fein and fancy find. Each is unique and (we can't resist) a good buy in this crewel world . . .

Annette Fein, Studio 51
51 Derech Hebron, Abu Tor
Jerusalem West
Phone: 711068, for
appointment
Hours: None special, but
especially not early
Dialogue in: English, Hebrew

BUTTON HOLE

From under the piles of old American Army riding breeches, old beaten British ammo belts with plenty of pockets, and khaki bags, small and large and in very good condition, considering some date back to 1918, Yitzhak produces bundles of buttons. But fabulous: Uncle Sam World War Twos emblazoned with eagles and stars; Mandate Palestine Police (PPs); Crowned Saudis; United Nations Officers; Australian Military Forces mapped with kangaroo country; Frenchy Foreign Legions... all of which he dashingly displays on large pieces of corrugated cardboard. Price-wise they are no rip-off, but they sure are different. Yitzhak also has some unidentifiables: buttons with crowns and some lettered "PHD"—a new way, perhaps, to drop your degree. These goodies are an alley scoop.

Yitzhak Something (he wouldn't tell)
51 Jaffa Road (alley near King George Street)
Downtown Jerusalem West
No phone (no anything)
Hours: 10–noon and 4–7; Friday till noon; closed Saturday
Dialogue in: Hebrew, Polish

Traditional Values

She was brought up on them, respects and perpetuates them in her embroidered interpretations of Jewish themes.
Malka Jagendorf does a flossy number. Traditional themes are loosely interpreted and tightly stitched in cotton or silk floss on linen, each with some wise words from the scriptures. It is an old Jewish custom.
I sent a letter to my love and on the way I flossed it:
Malka's mother's engagement gift to her father was a neatly needled Western Wall, and that was also Malka's original inspiration. She and her relatives in Mea Shearim are still in stitches as occasions arise, like a new home, a wedding, a birth. If you need a special-occasion gift, she will sew one, absolutely appropriate in subject and style.
Similarly traditional are her ceramic tiles. See them in her home. Malka is friendly, a pleasure to visit and makes you feel most welcome.
N.B. These facts are not embroidered upon.

Malka Jagendorf
22 Bourla Street, Apt. 8
Neve Granot (near Nayot),
Jerusalem West
Phone: 528128, to make sure she's in
Dialogue in: English, Hebrew, Yiddish, French and beginning Arabic

UNDER COVERS

It ain't like Paris, not even in the springtime, where the sewers are so super you can flee like Jean Valjean, the bishop's silver in your sack. Down ours you can barely roll a pearl. Small and skinny though they may be, Jerusalem does have a good graphic iron works covering the pipe, sewage, cable, water and phone works.

Y'acov Nuri is our undercover expert employed by the city lo these many years. He sports a finger ring, personally unearthed, and explains: the stone lids are Turkish, the English ovals are from the time of the British Mandate and the Arabic writ are of Jordanian rule.

His favorites are: (1) near the Jaffa Gate, 2 covers marked "PPW" with a diamond design—that's British for "Palestine Public Works"; (2) inside the Jaffa Gate, a stone lid perforated with small square holes—it's a rain drain and it's Turkish; and (3) round and all about town are "J WSs"—"Jerusalem Water Supply." It's all out there on the road, a kind of mini-municipal history. So what is "Cairo" doing on a Jaffa Road cover?

We rubbed them à la gravestones, and shot a few too. Herewith. Plus potentially alive, big, square peopleholes. Watch out.

The Grim Pill's Progress

homeopath is one who "treats diseases by minute doses of substances which would produce the disease in healthy persons" or, as Mr. Amnon Ozeransky, our happy homeo, says: "Like cures like" (homeo means "the same").

The story of O: he collects herbs in the hills of Jerusalem and in the Galilee, dries them and then prepares prescriptions using the herbs in specific concentrations. He also sells plain old dried herbs and the healthy stuff of life, like wheat germ made at the Monastery of the Abbey of the Fons. This is a straight and serious scene, as are the doctors who deal with him and in it.

If you are not into pill popping, as a hobby or lifestyle; if you are beyond chicken soup (the penicillin of the pale); or bugged by buba-meicyn (traditional Jewish antibiotic), you might give homeopathics a try. Honest.

Dictionary definition: a

Oplatka Pharmacy
110 Jaffa Road
Mahane Yehuda
Jerusalem West
Phone: 224021
Hours: 7:30–1 and 3–7;
Friday till 2, closed Saturday
Dialogue in: English, Hebrew,
Russian, Spanish, Yiddish,
German and Polish

55

There's one super-Orthodox medical clinic in town, organized by a group of women from the most religious Jewish neighborhoods and operated strictly according to biblical law.

In the densely populated areas in and around Mea Shearim, many people, for religious and financial reasons, could not or did not receive proper medical assistance.

What these women did: a clinic devoted to comfort, convenience and good medical care for those in the neighborhood. Toys for waiting children, religious books for waiting husbands in a separate room, a flower garden for everyone and plans for rock-bottom-priced prescriptions. Medical specialists from major Israeli hospitals donate their time and talent, and an ingroup spirit pervades.

Only four years old, the clinic has already helped four thousand families. The need is great; this idealistic center is financed completely by private donations. A worthy cause, and if this subject touches you, be an angel and get in touch with them:

Refoel Torah Jewry's
Medical Center
58 Shivtei Israel Street (next
to the pink and spired
Rumanian Orthodox
Patriarchate) (P.O.B. 5785)
Mea Shearim
Jerusalem West
Phone: 287754, 281727; ask
for Mr. A. H. Cohen, Info
Officer
Hours: Clinical
Dialogue in: Hebrew, Yiddish
English plus

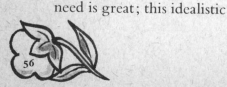

gift rapping

You can't find the shop where Martha got those fabulous earrings for next to nothing. You love the burnoose you bought for Babs and you know you won't be able to part with it once you're home. Your son-in-law, the meathead, wears an embroidered headband to the office, so you've got to find something farout for him. You can't find the shop Uncle Irving told you about, the one behind the *felafel* stand. You take another look at your "must-bring-a-present-to" list and shudder.

Take heart and take yourself up the musty staircase inside No. 2 Ben Yehuda Street. Hike up the two flights on the left set of stairs, turn right and right again. On the left will be a door marked "Magishay"— and you've made it. *Shay* means gift in Hebrew, and now Martha will get hers.

Something for everyperson, in-law or otherwise. Antique and modern jewelry of every type and cast: old copper and brass; new copper and brass; mirrors made from antique trays; plus charms, a collection of musty orange carnelian keyrings and lots by local artists. If it's not crowded, have a seat. You can swivel around and see a lot. The place is small, chock full, and the really nice salespeople will put their goods on the table for you, make suggestions, box and wrap.

Magishay Israeli Art Gifts
2 Ben Yehuda Street
Room 250
Downtown Jerusalem West
Phone: 222297, or home,
816913
Hours: 11–1 and 5–7; Friday
till 1; closed Saturday
Dialogue in: Hebrew, English,
Yiddish, Hungarian and
German

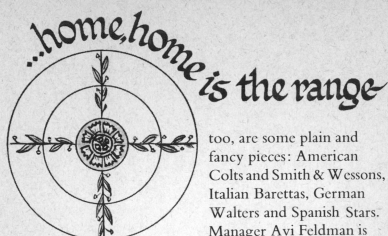

...home, home is the range

Not everyone is riding around the Wild West (Jerusalem) with a scimitar tucked under their robe. Many tuck licensed guns instead. For the scimitar swingers, there is always grass, as a last resort, on which to practice. But local pistol packers have never had a place to pop off. Now, this too, shall pass. Haim Yehezkely got his act together after paper shuffling for a year with the powers that be. He opened the first and only legal shooting gallery (10-meter range) in the midst of our serene surroundings.

S.W.S. is the place to practice, or take lessons with the live stuff. For sale, too, are some plain and fancy pieces: American Colts and Smith & Wessons, Italian Barettas, German Walters and Spanish Stars. Manager Avi Feldman is the (apparent) antithesis of the Mr. Macho we'd expected: well-spoken, courteous and knowledgeable. Although male customers exceed female, the latter number is gaining rapidly.

You may bring your own gun, and for a nominal fee you can shoot it out OK at their indoor corral.

*Security Watching System
(S.W.S.)
18 Rehov Ben Sira (near
Shlomzion Halmalka)
Jerusalem West
Phone: 223900
Hours: 8–1 and 4–7; Fridays
till 1; closed Saturdays
Dialogue in: Hebrew, English,
Yiddish, plus bits of Russian
and Arabic*

Women's Bib

A kind of "couching" called *tahariree* in Arabic—traditional Bethlehem hand embroidery done in pure silk or metallic (real gold if requested) thread and covering every square inch of elegant bib fronts for dresses, belts, collars, and zippered cushion covers with bright and beautiful designs. Beit Jalla-born Wadia Saleh is the madame in charge of the workshop for designing, cutting and sewing. If your current little black dress is a drag, bring it to her and she'll have it embroidered in the design you dig or decorate it herself with tiny olivewood beads. Or bring a picture and they'll reproduce in kind.

On display but not for sale are 70-year-old black Bedouin bridal robes ebulliently embroidered—breathtaking museumables.

Women's Association of Child's Care
Opposite St. Nicholas'
Church, Beit Jalla (hillside town just south of Jerusalem)
Phone: 8–12 and 1–5; closed Friday afternoon and Sunday Dialogue in: Arabic and a bit of English

FREUDIAN-FLIP

Until 2 years ago, Dr. Lesser was the only hypnotherapist in Jerusalem; now there are a couple of other sideliners. Through the hypnosis thing, which he learned in Germany but practiced mostly in the U.S., he is often able to cure symptoms and relieve pain. He does not cure the disease itself, a fact about which he is right up front. Can help some to stop smoking using the gradual-withdrawal method, as opposed to the old cold turkey bit. His patients present him with a mixed bag: homosexuality, family troubles, stuttering, impotence . . . and so it goes. An elderly man, almost 90, kindly and amiable. Depending on your degree of desperation, he may be worth a try.

Dr. Julius Lesser
34 Harlap Street, Kiryat
Shmuel, Jerusalem West
Phone: 64288, for appointment
Dialogue in: English,
German, "plus a little
French, Italian, Greek and
Latin"!

THE ✿ TOTAL ✿ TRIM
1&2

Bugged by buttons but need to close your jeans? Do them up with silver metal snaps, installed at the Avizar shop. Bring your own fabric and they'll cover buttons. Make button holes too. If you're feeling edgy, get off with their long line of trims: white eyelet to striped ruffled ribbon. Metal eyelets punched in, for a small fee, to emphasize your Heidi do. It's neat and new.

At last . . . striped suspenders, "Gents' Own," to be exact. Plus a plethora of buttons (even olive wood), lace and embroidered trims, fake fur pieces, sequins in all colors and sold by the thimble-full at 80 agorot per. To complete your total costume, Mr. Ibrahim T. Husseini offers oh-so-British black ties, white eyelet collars and garters and garter snaps, if you're into lace stockings. Reams of thread, rolls of grosgrain and satin ribbon, buckles and even fake flowers to decorate your hat, heart or cleavage.

Chic Avizar
3 Even Israel Street (just before the Brother Store, off Jaffa Road)
Downtown Jerusalem West
No phone
Hours: 8–1 and 3–7; Friday till 2; closed Saturday
Dialogue in: Arabic, Moroccan, French and Hebrew

Husseini
42 Salahadin Street (near the end of this main street, opposite St. George's Compound)
Jerusalem East
No phone
Hours: 10–1 and 3–6; Friday 3–6; closed Sunday
Dialogue in: Arabic and easy English

Love Locks

KETUBOT: Museum-style Jewish marriage contracts, a lost art reborn in Jerusalem and brainstormed by Janet, half of the underground-discovery duet. Poster-size frameables, richly colored on fine heavy vellum. Ideal wedding or anniversary gifts. The ancient text is rewrit in quintessential calligraphy with spaces to fill in the personal info. Accompanying English translation. Graphic stunners with the tender touch of loving biblical quotes. Exclusive at Maskit shops or write, Stateside, to:

Jerusalem Ketubot
105 Taconic Avenue
Great Barrington, Mass.
01230
Phone:(413) 528-4555

A Culinary Trip

Get *The Flavor of Jerusalem*, as well as the color and texture and taste of our town, in a trip of a novel new cookbook. The favorite recipes and personal vignettes of some of our most colorful Jerusalemites. Non-sectarian. Not strictly kosher. Non-fictional. A foody, fun way to the heartbeat here.

Get it at *Steimatzky's* purveyor of anything and everything in print on the subject of Jerusalem, and Israel; seller of books, back-home newspapers, magazines and maps for the last 52 years; shops in downtown Zion Square and hotel lobbies.

The Flavor of Jerusalem
By Joan Nathan & Judy Stacey Goldman, Foreword by Mayor Teddy Kollek Little, Brown and Company

The Flavor of Jerusalem

**Joan Nathan and
Judy Stacey Goldman**

**Foreword by
Mayor Teddy Kollek**

International recipes from the
many cuisines of the sacred city

(Private) Eye Shadow

Some three years ago Simon Azulai was in a lawyer friend's office where he heard the sad tale of Mrs. X., whose husband had x-ited and not returned. Mr. Azulai had a feeling that he could help and so he said, "How much will you give me if I find him?" "Four hundred pounds" was the answer (that was before *the* devaluation). He found Mr. X in four hours and has been detecting ever since.

"It's simple," says Simon. "You just have to be a *nudnik*; you have to like people and be interested in them and be of strong character." Simon has no training as a policeman (which might or might not help) and is sure he's the only person doing this work who was never a boy in blue.

Background: Wounded during the Sinai Campaign, he pushed himself to excel in all sports, became a karate and judo expert, runs 20 kilometers a day, swims across the Sea of Galilee in the yearly competition and has a license from the Ministry of Justice to do detecting. His private investigations not only dig up dropouts. He also checks on strays, strays after checks, collects fines and fees and will even get into personal problems such as those arising between bad neighbors. Has no gun (that we know of), but will travel, anywhere in the country and at a moment's notice, and people from all over come to him.

Simon Azulai
Office of Private Investigation
10 Ben Yehuda Street
Downtown Jerusalem West
Hours: 4:30–6:30
Phone: 234136, or leave a message on the recorder, 418035
Dialogue in: Hebrew, Arabic, a little English and German

On the Safe Side

. . . of Wadi Joz Street, that is. In the middle of this irregular block and before the big blue VW sign, Suliman Shawer's sign reads:
"SAFE MANUFACTURERS AND TENDER BODIES."
Him we had to investigate. Suliman makes iron safes, all sizes and shapes, by special order, in only a month or so. He can install a wee one for precious hideaways or set you up with a showy biggy. (Socioeconomic note: the more robberies, the busier business—and lately his business is a boom.)
You may also be casting about for a tender body (aren't we all), but in Israel, a "*tender*" is a type of small truck, so the *entendre* is triple.

S.S. is happy, handsome, helpful and hospitable.

Suliman Shawer
23 Wadi Joz Street
East of Jerusalem East
Hours: 7:30–5 (except for lunch, 12–12:30); closed Sunday
Dialogue in: Arabic, Hebrew, and 50% English"

the tarbush wacker

Beat it babe—here comes the fuzz! Nope, it's the fez! And you thought it was The Graduate because there's a black tassle on his hat.

Friends, you have seen an astounding array in the local hat parade of our sacred city: skullcaps, *kaffiyehs*, hoods, panamas, priestly conicals and flat-tops, fur-trimmed *shtreimels*, bonnets, berets, and bowlers. And now . . . The Fez!

"Fez" is a Maghrebi word for *tarbush*, which is an Arabic word for an inverted flowerpot-shaped hat, rimless and tassled. It is worn to symbolize one's having made it to Mecca, the ultimate aim of a religious pilgrimage, and Mr. Abruk is the last one whacking them out. He has been molding his maroon felt (imported from Czechoslovakia) into fezes

for the last 22 years, on his own Egyptian brass fez forms. After him, who knows? No one else in town is initiate to the fey art of the fez. Better buy one to be one of the first among the last.

Philipe Abruk
Greek Orthodox Patriarchate
Street (about 5 doors up on the right)
Old City
No phone
Hours: 8–6 with lunchbreaks; closed Sunday
Dialogue in: Arabic, Turkish, English, Persian, Armenian

the WELDERS of ZION

For super-scavengers and handy householders: the iron-ies of life, wrought and otherwise, are here for you, en masse and al fresco, side by side, piled up and under, over and in-between. Old balcony railings (to maybe head your bed), milk cans, gates, fence sections, window frames, chains (for swingers) and even bathtubs. All manner of by-gone building materials to be re-used per your imagination. If you are really on your mettle, you might find a brassy old lamp or chandelier. Prices go according to weight and/or workmanship. Heavy scene here: prepare for use of muscle, lots of legwork and dirty hands.

Nurit & Eliahu Mizrachi's Machsan ("Storeroom") 18 Israel Najara Street Givat Shaul, Jerusalem West Phone: 523524 Hours: 8–4; Friday till 1; closed Saturday Dialogue in: Hebrew

Metal Spinning

Raphael and Shemtov Marchaim have been spinning off metalworks in their dark little factory in the same spot since 1951— even when it was within paper-airplane range of the Jordanian border. Turkish born, they learned their craft as apprentices before coming to Israel, many moons ago.

From all manner of metals, (silver, brass, aluminum, chrome, gold and platinum) they make the basics of things like trays, wine cups and candlesticks which are then assembled and decorated elsewhere. Inside their old wooden doors, the shelves are piled high with sheets and circles of undone metal, then to be spun into shape on their handmade wooden or metal forms. An Old World art, and they are Onlies in Jerusalem. For bulk buying and big quantity orders.

Merchaim Brothers
16 Eliahu Shama Street
(off King David Street on
your track into town, way
down to the end. Across from
the paper shredders whose
stuff spills onto the street)
Jerusalem West
Phone: 226589
Hours: 8:30–4:30; Friday
till 1:30; closed Saturday
Dialogue in: Hebrew,
Turkish, Ladino

# THOUSE

... and garden. A family-type silk-screen factory which turns out quality Tee-shirts with kooky and custom-made slogans. Best sellers are the Coca-Colas emblazoned in Hebrew on every color, plus Dry Bones "Protexias," Super Goldas, and Shaloms—all of high caliber and for good, low prices. Better yet, have your own thing done: for a fatter fee, a custom-designed one-of-a-kind T- or sweat shirt to display your endless extravagant ego. Or order a bulk to proclaim your tour, team, club or family clan.

Two enterprising young Englishmen, Jonathan Lubell and William White, provide the brains and brawn behind this new company. They are multi-talented and very hip.

Pop-pow posters, irreverent and whimsical, are also available ... Lots of light-weight gifts to go.

Lillit T-Shirts
28 Efrata
Talpiot, Jerusalem West
Phone: 262851
Dialogue in: English, Hebrew

Ancient Artyfacts

In his eyrie office above the reproductions workshop, Abraham Levy has a consummate collection of real antiquities: 2,000-year-old Roman glass, Bronze Age pieces, 5,000 year-old pottery. One of his wonders is a collection of ancient beads which he strings up into wearable jewelry. For a little over $100 you can deck your neck in a Bronze Age necklace, and each ancient bead costs only a few pennies per year old. Other-era neckables: Islamic glass and Ottoman silver, sometimes with ear doodads to match.

A knowledgeable and creative collector, Mr. L. will brainstorm special gifts by subject matter, e.g., a boxed set of ancient surgeon's implements, pre-biblical fisherman's gear, ancient bells or Yigael Yadin's book *Massada* boxed together with some actual finds described therein.

No less fabulous than his collection is his clientele: international luminaries from presidents to prime ministers, a couple of cardinals and even the Pope himself.

A second specialty is executive gifts created in the workshop below, overseen by wife, Chana. Very good repros of ancient oil lamps, coins, *menorahs* and all manner of gifts that can be personalized with your organization's name.

Abraham & Chana Levy
Antiquities of the Holy Land
9 Alkabez Street, Givat
Shaul, Jerusalem West
(Second left off the main road.
Across the street from Blue
Band Margarine, under an
arch and past a coal bin)
Phone: 526602
Hours: 8–2; Friday till 1;
closed Saturday
Dialogue in: Hebrew, English,
German, French, Arabic

73

A BOX ON THEE

Israelis, fluffs up his income with a second job. He carves mulberry-wood boxes—seamless, primitive squares and pointed ovals—and then he decorates them with bits of scrap metal.

His lifestyle—the rusty red garden gate, the hill, the house, his p.j. costume—the whole scene is a magic-carpet trip straight from Yemen. Please do not visit Mr. Hebebeh just for the joy of it unless you are willing to buy a box. Only about IL 80 and definitely worth the trip of the treck.★

Shalom Hebebeh
90 Ezore Bet (Area B)
Ein Karem
★The Treck: near the last bus stop in E.K., turn down the path near the red fire hydrant (avoid any and all paved roads in view), walk down into the wadi *and up to the third gate. Stoney and dusty*
A knockout view.
No phone
Dialogue in: Arabic and delicate Hebrew

Of all the Jerusalem cliff-hangers we have come to know and love, Mr. Hebebeh is the most marvelous. He came from Yemen to live in Israel, and live he does, on the inside of a hillside in the *wadi* (dry riverbed) of our arty suburb village, Ein Kerem.
Mr. H. works as a *sandlar* (shoemaker) but, like most

different folks have

Best in ballpoint, but break out your magic marker, pencil or pen for a serious and sensational psyche-out. You can't fool or sidetrack Shaul by writing b.s. because "it's not what you write, but *h o w*." He's a great graphologist, first-rate, and uses his science to help potential employers read between the applicants' lines (like in banks or security work). He deciphers in detective deals too.

On a personal level, he reads your future and parts of your past from how you write. Show him your hands and he analyzes character. It's the feel of fortune.

No gentler Jerusalemite could you entrust, kindly and calm. Potential tragedies (heaven forbid) he does not tell. Shaul has been reading write-offs for 10 years, first as a hobby. Now he free-lances for the folding stuff, and he's right on.

Shaul Halili
28 Kore Hadorot, Apt. 17
(fabulous view)
Talpiot, Jerusalem West
Phone: 262007 after 1 p.m.
for appointment
Dialogue in: Hebrew, Arabic,
Spanish, very elementary
English (so bring a
trustworthy native)

different Strokes

A Rummage Tale

"The Official Arrival of General Allenby at the Holy City" . . . "The Pool of Hezekiah, Jerusalem, Palestine" . . . "The Duke of Connaught on His Way to the Holy Sepulchre" . . . "The Jews Wailing Place on Friday" . . . "Water Carriers in the Mosque of Omar Court-Yard." All *sic*. All sensational. All from 1917–1921. These are the captions of *circa*-60-year-old historical (some hysterical) photos captured forever in curious yellow on authentic old Palestine postcards. Yours to mail or frame or just love.

Mr. Rittas, himself frameable and loveable, has hoards of these plus a houseful of every other kind of thing: tons of trinketry, coins, worry beads, buttons, Greek incense, Italian tie tacks, olive-wood walking canes, stamps, scarabs, Bethlehem beads, icons jammed and crammed into corners and old books in old world languages.

He is a grand old Greek who came here on a pilgrimage over 50 years ago and stayed. He wants only to "see peace come to the Holyland," having seen and lived through so much of the opposite. He'll tell you about that, and about how he once sent a carved camel to General Eisenhower with his message for peace, and about the gifts he has sent to other famous people, and about . . .

The Little Museum
Corner of St. Dimitri Road
and the Greek Orthodox
Patriarchate Road, Old City
(Second left from Jaffa Gate,
turn and follow the curves)
No phone
Hours: Not exact, around 9–1
and 4–8; closed Sunday
Dialogue in: Greek, English,
French, Hebrew, Arabic,
German and a little Italian

BOOB TUBES

Mind your macho—here's the only female "puncture macher*" in the Middle East! Esther Gassner and some of her eight children (especially 2 daughters) balance, sell, repair, and recap tires like nobody's business.

Mother makes the scene amid huge rubbery plants (each has its own story), a kitchen where customer coffee awaits, and a treadle sewing machine for overall repairs. But the real master is the miss—daughter Chana—well-known for tireless efforts at the tender age of twenty-two. A serious, responsible family setup. Pithy parables at no extra charge, plus real cream in your coffee.

*a doer

*Gassner Brothers, Tyres
1 Tuval Street,
Industrial Center, Romema
Jerusalem West
Phone: 524515
Hours: 7–4; Friday till 2;
closed Saturday
Dialogue in: English, Hebrew,
German, Yiddish, Arabic*

Cinderseller

The Perils of Palestine as told on July 4th: Red, White and Blue, and I want a barbecue. Hot dogs, spare ribs and hamburgers too. But here I am, without my power-operated, family-size, hickory-seasoned, copper-hooded, brick-faced Super-Grill. What to do? Wait for Uncle Sam to bring one under his madras sport jacket? Too long. He's not coming until El Al offers charter flights.

So I jump into my "Sousita" (Israeli-made car, the name means horse) and blast off to Mahane Yehuda to Simon Hutta's stall. He supplies me with a bag of charcoal (cindery but OK), skewers for kebabs (local substute for hot dogs) and an Israeli "bar-b-q") (an oblong aluminum box with bars on top).

Simon Says he's an expert pewter mender and lamp fixer, too.

Simon Hutta
4 Ha'agas Street
Mahane Yehuda (his hut is across from No. 18 Mahane Yehuda Street, which is the main street in this outdoor market)
Jerusalem West
No phone
Hours: All
Dialogue in: Hebrew

up Against The Wool

If you happen to be up before sunrise and it happens to be a Friday and you happen to turn the corner past Herod's Gate onto Jericho Road, you will happen upon a wild and woolly event up against the outer wall of the Old City. Every Friday morning, a live sheep sale takes place, sometimes cows, goats, and horses too.

Sheep are sold according to weight (average cost is about IL 500 these days). A pregnant goat costs about IL 900, and the best riding horse, imported from the Negev, goes for about IL 4,000. A note on bargaining style: you, as buyer, don't ask the price. Make your offer. Beware. Be tough. And handhold throughout (conventional here—not kinky).

Even if you are not in the market for a live one, the black-robed Bedouin, the shepherds, the soft sunrise, the dust puffs, plus the wee woollies all make for a great photographic high.

Listen for "Ba-a-a-a" and Other Sounds of Furry.
Southeast Corner,
Old City Outside Wall
Jerusalem East
Hours: 5 a.m. to early mid-morn, Fridays only
Dialogue: mostly in non-verbal universals, but bone up on your Arabic numerals beforehand

the Beautiful Brush-off

Va...va...va...broom! Blast off in your Benz and zoom up the Mountain Scopus. Look for big red valentine hearts painted on monster metal gates. Inside are scrubbies for us grubbies: brushes for dishes, floors, walls, white-washing and paint. And once the rush is over, zero in on the wicker: curlicue carpet beaters, waste baskets, laundry hampers, stools, tables, and chairs. Even wicker for your wedding: tiny baskets to fill with candies for your sweet guests.

Every part of every piece is handmade, from bristle to broom stick, and it's all done by men who work in the Lutheran World Federation Workshop for the Blind. They are taught on the premises, and their work is lovingly done and handily crafted—a cause worthy of a revel.

Lutheran World Federation Mount Scopus, Jerusalem East (At the top of the road to the Intercontinental Hotel, turn left to Mount Scopus. On the right, watch for hearty gates) Phone: 282903 Hours: 7–12 and 1–4; Saturday till 1; closed Sunday Dialogue in: Ask for Fuad Mussalam. He speaks English and Arabic

82

AYE HERE'S THE RUB

Knotty knees? Curled-up calves? Getting older? Bursitis bolder? Tensed-up shoulder?

Let Miriam rub it out. After all, she's been massaging since she was ten years old. You must bring your own sheet (leave the Yves St. Laurent at home, take the *alte shmata*). You may partake of a general "health" massage or a specific "pains" massage. Question: Miriam, can you tell our readers if their pains will pass after one of your massages? Answer: "I do not sign a contract! But doctors, lawyers and professors come to me, so you can too."

See why we love her? And her formica-fabulous home is spotless, mother-in-law-clean, and tucked into the Yemenite quarter, the cleanest in the city.

Miriam Badicha
21 Zippori Street, corner Even Sapir
Yemenite Quarter, Jerusalem West
Phone: 233692, for appointment
Dialogue in: Hebrew, Arabic, laying on of hands

TRUE GRITS

Guess what's in the German Colony. A German winery, of course, built in 1875. And you guessed it: they're making whitewash in the old winery. Vat else?! The other specialty is white sand, brought to you by those wonderful folks who brought us our Mediterranean seashore. Clean, sifty, shifty sand to upgrade your box. Or for your curving driveway there are lovely little stones, i.e., gravel (Gertie would love them) in beige, white or grey-pink, depending on what old block they are chips off.

Erdman & Sons (David is the one there)
13 Emek Refaim (opposite the International Cultural Center for Youth)
German Colony
Jerusalem West
Phone: 31605
Hours: 7–4; Friday till 1:30; closed Saturday
Dialogue in: Hebrew, Arabic and English

Bio Batik

How do you express yourself? Yeah, well, me too. Alexandra, however, says it in batik. Her grandfather was one of the country's first Zionists and one of Israel's famous first settlers. (His house in Tivon is now a landmark; there's also a statue of him on horseback.) Many of Alexandra's batiks express scenes of her childhood and family memories. One of the most charming is a wall hanging of her and her sister atop their horse in front of grandfather's house.

Alexandra does her batik biographicals in a backyard studio, a tree sticking into her window. Pow-pow pillow covers with zippers; wall hangings ready to go up; special batiks for children's rooms with lots of detail "so they'll keep interested"; dress lengths with the design specially placed to fit your front; ready-mades too. All are on cotton, but silk can be specially ordered.

Alexandra Zaid
59 Ussishkin Street
Jerusalem West
Phone: 226343
Hours: 9–1; call first for
afternoon visits
Dialogue in: Hebrew, English

A HELPING HAND

The *hamsa*, ubiquitous
Mideast amulet for good
luck, is an open hand, and
Ohana's collection is great:
giant ones for walls and
tiny ones for jewelry.
Upside-down they protect
from the evil eye and
downside-up bring mazel.
Lucky you! Young and
handsome (at the time of
this writing), Moroccan-
born Mr. O. can offer
other styles of amulets too,
some inscribed with
prayers for peace and some
with hosannas for heroism.
Mostly silver, old and
new.
Bye bye, evil eye . . .

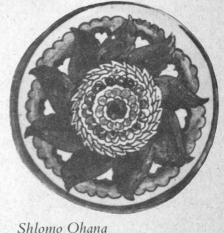

Shlomo Ohana
20 Ein Yaakov Street (near
the Petit Musee)
Mea Shearim
Jerusalem West
No phone
Hours: 9–7; Friday till 3;
closed Saturday
Dialogue in: French, Arabic,
Hebrew and a little English.

the razz tattoo

In the back room of the Green Valley Salon (a barbershop), Mr. Razzouk will do you a tattoo that only lasts forever. A sweet old man, *circa* 70, Mr. Razzouk's own arm was decorated by his dad 60 years ago.

The sign says, "Electric Tattoo with Colors and Modern Machines." We investigated: the "modern machines" consist of an electric needle, and the choice of colors: dark blue or dark blue.

On his wall is a selection of tattoos from which to choose: St. George and Jesus are the most in demand, but the Star of David is rising fast.

Who takes to tattoos? Pilgrims, Moslems, Christians and Jews. The Bedouin get it on their own tribal grounds. Radical female chic now instructs: a tiny tattoo on your ankle, shoulder, or gentle curve of your . . .

Pain: minimal (by hear-say only).

Wadia Razzouk
18 Aqabat el-Khanka Street
Old City (At the end of Christian Quarter Street, turn right, on and down a bit)
No phone, but his neighbor's, Ramadan Hirbawi, is 280904
Hours: 8–5; closed Sunday
Dialogue in: Arabic only

Rubber Man

Rubber stamps in any and every language, with or without your personal logo design—office style with crummy plastic handles or pocket style in cute chrome cases. A neat (as in immaculate) upstairs place in one of Jerusalem's oldest neighborhoods.

Mr. Rubberman is amiable, helpful and patient. Burly of bod, Turkish born, he delivers fast. Select your type type from his orderly pile of little school-style notebooks—themselves a kind of history of Jerusalem. He's stamped for everyone, all government ministries, businesses, very VIPs.

Plus some unexpecteds: like a stamp for the "Guardians of the Wailing Wall" and one for Rachel's Tomb.

N.B.: From his office window is a visual shotline direct to the No. 18 bus stop (affectionately known as the Streetcar Named Perspire). Local color at the pinnacle of its passion. Observe how an Israeli line (queue) is formed!

Kadima Chotamot ("Quick Stamps") 35 Jaffa Road Downtown Jerusalem West (Down the little lane, first right into courtyard, under an arch marked "2" and left, up, up and around the slippery stone steps)
Phone : 234813
Hours: 8:30–1 and 3–6:30; Friday till 1, closed Saturday
Dialogue in: Hebrew, Ladino

91

A Touch Of Glass

A tree grows in Neker's—right through the roof and on past the shelves of gifty glassware: candle holders, juglets, ash trays, stoppered perfume bottles, vases and more.

Father Neker and his 3 sons resettled from Baghdad to blow glass in the peace and quiet of their workshop home. They also make all their own glazes from secret formulas.

There's nothing hush-hush, however, about the hot bright colors they produce. A second spectrum is their other line of iridescent, pearly pastels. All this and a giftbox too (a touch not always available in many retail stores).

Repairs when possible. Reproductions by special order. Take advantage of factory prices and the pleasure of seeing the magical blowing process if you're keen to.

Neker Glass Factory
6 Beit Israel Street
(opposite Mirrer Yeshiva)
Mea Shearim
Jerusalem West
Phone: 286683
Hours: 8–4:30 with lunch
breaks; Friday till 2;
closed Saturday
Dialogue in: Hebrew, Arabic,
and English

93

AN ISOSCELES TO EAT

Nothing says "lovin'" like something from the oven, especially when someone else is doing the baking. *Burekas* are flaky pastries triangled around a filling of either spinach or cheese. Hadassa Pinhassi prepares them at home and then bakes and sells them in her homey restaurant. Melt-in-the-tummy yummy.

So comb the curls out of your eyes. Smile. Hold it. Say "c-h-e-e-s-e," or "spinach"—whichever you prefer. Eat at the window of her tiny coffee bar or step inside to join the regulars who are loving them, and her and themselves.

Our stoolside companion ordered two (one of each) plus a café au lait and a brandy. What better way to start the workaday? Cheaper if eaten outside, and if ordered for parties, even cheaper by the dozens.

Mifgash Menora ("Meet at the Menorah")
7 Bezalel Street, corner Hagidem (beside Houminer's Hardware)
Jerusalem West
Phone: 228510
Hours: 7–7; Friday till 2; closed Saturday
Dialogue in: Hebrew

The X factor in this story is the cross-stitch, deftly done by Arab village women on locally woven cloth. It is a traditional type of embroidery. The designs are done in all colors, but blue, green and brown are best. Tablecloths and runners, placemats, napkins, pillow covers, knitting bags, guest towels, aprons, baby bibs, dress lengths, etcetera.

The center is sponsored and and supported by the Mennonites and is the showcase for work assigned to women in remote villages. You are helping a woman supplement her family income when you buy here. Help a Woman, you'll feel good.

The Arab Needlework Shoppe
Jerusalem East
(From downtown East
Jerusalem, take the road to
Ramalla; it's across from the
Ambassador Hotel)
Phone: 282833
Hours: 8–1 and 3–5;
Saturday 10–4; closed Sunday
Dialogue in: Arabic,
light Hebrew and English

Loofas and Goofas

LOOFAS are little scrubbers knitted from soft, hairy twine into loopy, lacey, double-thick circles. Use in your ablutions, ritual or kinky. But if you don't like to scrub in your tub, use them decoratively as ethnic art. Best to buy where and when they're

being made—hot off the needles, like:
On Mahane Yehuda Street (the outdoor market) where you can watch 3 or 4 tough old men squatting at their personal sidewalk stakeouts and knitting up these semi-softies; or
On the bench in Zahal Square in front of the bagel-baker (see "Flour Power," page 133) where a little old loofa lady sits and knits a lot. She's there almost every day.

GOOFAS are black buckets made from old automobile tires, soft and strong (the way we like 'em). They're used throughout The Land to send the soil from under to above ground on digs, archaeological or otherwise. You can stick a pot of hot-pink geraniums in your goofa or use one as a charcoal bin near your b-b-q. Buy them around in the Old City and/or Mahane Yehuda. The local supply is usually in great demand, so good goofa luck.

Holywood

Israel Hershkovitz and his Hungarian-born father have a tiny shop where they make Jewish ceremonial items out of beechwood imported from Europe: *havdalah* spice boxes, Passover *matzot* trays, Torah scroll handles, and *megillah* cases. (He also engraves on silver.) Everything inside is covered with wood curls, including the craftymen.

Son Hershkovitz explained that they used to do a good business making *mezzuzah* cases, but since the Six-Day War, 90% of those on the market are produced from olive wood in Bethlehem.

Most of their work is by special order. They have a real old-style woodsy touch, one that ensures getting what you want and what you pay for.

J. Hershkovitz, Wood–Turner
14 Zonnenfeld Street
Mea Shearim, Jerusalem West
No Phone
Hours: 9–4; closed Saturday
Dialogue in: Hebrew,
German, 5 brands of Yiddish

The Avant Underground

From the caves and pits of our ethnic entries, we now turn around to how the other half makes it. We proudly present (ta *TAH*) Sara Gilat, whose cave is the basement of her very varoom villa.

Hung up down there are some of the bravest new world artworks (paintings and sculptures). Sara likes to promote young and/or undiscovered Israeli artists, but she also shows the way-out well-knowns, domestic and imported.

Ms. Gilat is most knowledgeable plus Come-to-Israel poster pretty: dark haired and dusky eyed. She sometimes invites people upstairs to her living rooms, which are Beyond Bloomingdale's stunning. Hung up, up there, are more paintings and prints, some for sale, some for show.

Sara Gilat
4 Pinsker Street (near the Jerusalem Theater), Talbieh
Jerusalem West
Phone: 64121
Hours: 4–6 daily except Friday and Saturday
Dialogue in: English, Hebrew, French and a little German

Splendor in the Glass

The Romans really knew how to live, lying around on couches, flipping figs, tripping around in togas and all. They lived and loved in many lands, and when they were here, they left us the most fabulous frosty pearl glass.

Uri Ramot takes 2000-year old chunklets of iridescent Roman glass, beautiful blues and gorgeous greens, and frames them in 18-karat gold to fashion splendiferous pendants, pins, buckles and earrings.

The glory that was Rome can now be yours. Uri captured it and his own tunes of glory are now being tooted internationally. His works are selected as gifts by and for the greatest: Henry the K got one; Artur Rubinstein too. We met Uri in his apartment-workshop, but by now you'll see him everywhere, in Maskit, in his new studio at Khutzot Hayotser, and heaven knows . . .

Very high quality. High but worth-it prices, and exceedingly exclusive.

Uri Ramot
6 Lev Yaffe Street, Talpiot
Jerusalem West
Phone: 262617
Hours: By appointment
Dialogue in: Hebrew,
Yiddish, English

A person really has to be rugged to set up and sit down to work outdoors on any main street. Practicing your profession on Jerusalem's busy Ben Yehuda, however, takes courage above and beyond the call. Stamina too. But day after day, all year round, here she is, Mazal Mizrachi (known and loved by all as "the carpet lady"), serenely stitching away and rebinding rugs at knee level on the city's busiest walkway. Every morning she wheels her small cart down Jaffa Road and over to her spot in front of Stock's (an exclusive women's wear store). Here she unloads her workshop: a tiny stool, bundles of yarn, a couple of tough needles, the carpets she is currently mending, and a cardboard sign giving her name and profession, which she places beside her. Mrs. Mizrachi arrived here in 1938 from Persia. Now she's 58, white-haired, cherry-cheeked, busy, beautiful and hearty.

Mazal Mizrachi
3 Ben Yehuda Street (near Zion Square, on the sidewalk)
Downtown Jerusalem West
Phone: 229922 (home)
Hours: 10–1 and never on Saturday
Dialogue in: Hebrew, Arabic, and a little Spanish

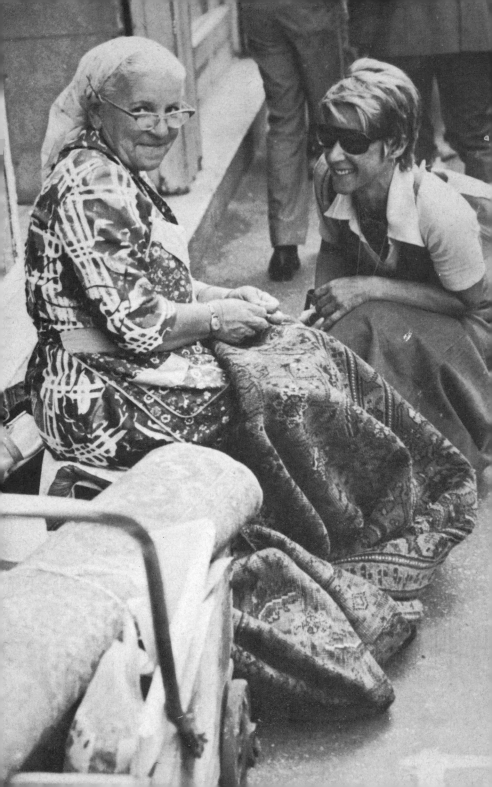

Neo-Bedouin Camp

You'd expect maybe the tent-maker of Jerusalem to be sandalled and swarthed, nose ring glinting in the sun, sipping coffee under a fabulously flapped tent. You'd also expect his name to be Omar. So much for great expectations. Bulgarian-born Nissim Abramov is who our tent-maker is, and he is the only one around, except for his nextdoor neighbor, who sews canvas but does not make tents. Nissim sits behind his industrial sewing machine, sipping a glass of tea with its steadily soaking tea bag, and zips off all kinds of canvas covers. Tents for army and fun, beach umbrellas, car cocoons (you gotta live here to get it), plus knapsacks and tote bags, in blazing saddle solids and stripes. Repairs too.

Abrizent Tents
9 Mamilla Street
Jerusalem West
Phone: 231626
Hours: 8–5 without a break
(he eats in); Friday till 2;
closed Saturday
Dialogue in: Hebrew,
Bulgarian

farout from the maddening crowd

"Too stoned in Ein Kerem, she left for Mea Shearim." That was the sign on Hortense's shop on Main Street, where she used to sell the remains of a 5000-kilo load of silk parasols, clunk junk jewelry, odd old crystal, peacock feathers, boas, shells, etcetera. Much more fascinating, however, are her oil paintings, luminous and mystical in subject and style.

Her lease ran out, so out she went to sell her paintings in the Mea Shearim market, on the sidewalk. Ask around, or look for Hortense in the afternoons. She wears a black skull scarf that ends at her knees and is a member of the Neturei Karta, the extremist Jewish sect which does not recognize the State of Israel. Hortense was born in Alsace into an old rabbinical family. She traveled around the world, lived through the Holocaust, lived in India, studied law and is a professional painter. To get the *gestalt* between the sign, the scarf and the sect, you'll have to coax her to explain.

Hortense (pseudonym)
Main Street in Mea Shearim
market
No Phone
Hours: Afternoons; never on
Saturday
Dialogue in: French, fair
English

> HORTENSE
>
> Pseudonym of a French-born, from an old Alsacian rabbinical family self-taught painter-a previous lawyer—
>
> Auschwitz—and a round-tour, main with a stay in India, in her curriculum vitae—
>
> Too stoned in wonderful Ein-Karem, she has left for the orthodox quaerter of Mea-Shearim where she devotes lherself to paint religious subjects
>
> She started self-selling in her own antiquilies shop, named the "VASE DE SOISSONS"—
>
> Husband ben-Yeshiva—a small boy—

Little Women

. . . but not the saccharine storybook type. Lea Mintz Majara is an artist with an absolutely distinctive style and message.

Most of her collection is naked women—of all sizes but with one thematic shape: heavy hips, hollow bellies, and big breasts. Although she started her career as a painter, she began to sculpt after the Six-Day War to express the anguish of the times in which we lived. After it was safe enough to leave the shelter where she stayed with her two young sons, Lea began to translate her fears and the dread she shared with all women. "Women pour out their insides bearing children and feel empty if separated from them."

She has some fabulously complicated and creative displays, including a permanent exhibit of "White Tombs", which consists of 8 individual scenes, and some densely populated "Crowds," which she will be pleased to discuss.

Although she does not sell the works to which she is sentimentally attached, prices on other pieces range from IL 150 to IL 5,000.

Lea's family has lived in Jerusalem for over 200 years, and if you can finally find her in the renovated area of the Jewish Quarter, she will welcome you to to see her terra cotta women—all displayed in the white catacombs, coves, arches and winding halls of her home. And don't miss her rooftop either.

Lea Mintz Majara
56 Misgav Ladach Street
Jewish Quarter, Old City
(With your back to Rothschild House, walk diagonally across the courtyard to the left, down the stone steps and ask)
Hours: 11–2, plus by appointment
Dialogue in: Hebrew, English, French and Arabic; she understands German too

THE JOY OF HEX

If you are not a boutique owner or a trendy businessperson, skip this story.

A former morning-mail delivery woman, and now a young mother, Sharona bead-embroiders the most fantasmagraphic designs ever. On a visit to Haiti, she was bitten by the voodoo bug, and the ceremonial flags inspired her to star spangle a few for herself.

No appointments are available, and her studio-gallery-home is not open to the public. Sharona's master plan is to work up a couple of dozen weirdo wonders and present them to the public in one dazzling array. Are you Bobby Dazzler? or the Philadelphia Flasher?

Sharona Nathan
3 Boaz Street (We promised not to tell, but you'll never find it anyway)
No phone
No hours
Dialogue in: Hebrew, English

Bossa Nava

THE LIVING END

"Let them eat cake!" said Ms. Antoinette as she pulled her corset strings tighter. The motto: Nothing strained, nothing gained.

If you'd like to see your gain on the wane, check in at Café Nava's cake counter on Tuesdays—the day they bake cakes and cookies which are sugar- and cyclamate-free. Come between 11 and 12 noon for the best choice, which includes sponge, chocolate, nut, cheese and apple.

Café Nava
44 Jaffa Road (near Zion Square)
Downtown Jerusalem West
Phone: 222861
Dialogue in: Hebrew, English, French, Yiddish, Polish, Rumanian, Hungarian

Boulous ("The Bull") is a carpenter who carves in a cave with green wooden doors with a nonsequitur sign that advertises tattoos.

If you are dying to go in, you'll find a cave full of coffins and Boulous doing his thing from the beginning for the bitter end. Fully finished, and complete with satin pillow, his coffins go for about IL 800, and up…

Boulous
Corner of Christian Quarter Street & St. Francis St.
Old City
No Phone
Hours: Daytime
Dialogue in: Arabic

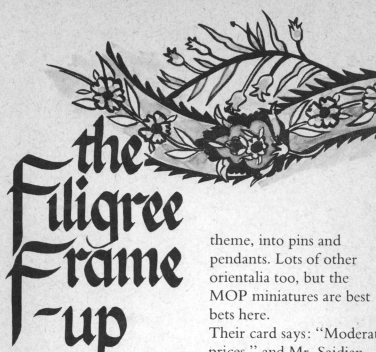

the filigree frame-up

Forty years ago, Mr. Rabbi (he's not) Saidian exodused from Iran, bringing with him a weird and wonderful collection of hand-painted, mother-of-pearl miniature pictures—all sizes and shapes, even hearts and ducks. In his on-the-spot workshop, son Yedidia makes the delicate sterling filigree frames that transform these tiny pictures, often biblical in theme, into pins and pendants. Lots of other orientalia too, but the MOP miniatures are best bets here.

Their card says: "Moderate prices," and Mr. Saidian says: "I tell the truth." What can we tell you— his Persian minis are mucho.

The Petit Musee
16 Ein Yaakov Street (near the Yeshiva Building in the market square), Mea Shearim Jerusalem West
No phone
Hours: 10–7; Friday till 3; closed Saturday
Dialogue in: French, English, Hebrew, Arabic, plus 2 dialects of Persian

talis man

An outdoor grey-bearded rabbi with a big white smile. He sits on the ledge between Wizo and the bank, and next to him are packets of his paper prayers wrapped around with string.

He kisses the charms (called *camayahs* in Hebrew) that will protect you from evil spirits, cure your any ache and attract good luck according to your personal need. Or forget your woes for a while and enjoy watching the variety of city strollers who line up for advice and blessings.

Inside each little packet are mysterious abbreviated invocations, including a square little *hamsa*-hand for double insurance. There's nothing mystical, however, about his pricing system. Each is marked right out front on the title flap. The order of purchase is: untie, unfold, kiss, pray, then pay.

Rabbi Yitzhak Nissim is an old Baghdadi, here 1/2 a century and a 1-man institution in town.

Rabbi Yitzhak Nissim
Jaffa Road near Queen
Helene Street
Jerusalem West
Hours: Mornings
Dialogue in: Clunky Hebrew

Edible Complex

What's a birthday cake without silver sprinkles? Or Chinese food without ginger root? Or coffee without Melita filters? Or hair without henna? William Khoury's shop has all the above and also the below: every unbelievable spice, glazed cherries, custom-blended curry powder, *kizha* (to sprinkle on cheese), ground anise and kimmel, plus bird seed, dried fruits, food-coloring powders, birthday cake candles and holders, even bride-and-groom dolls for the festive W. cake. Kit Kat's specialty is all kinds of coffee, roasted on the premises and ground to your heart's desire. He can grind the *hell* (Arabic for cardamon) right into your Turkish beans. Courteous and kind, Mr. K. knows all and will tell all if you have questions concerning local yokel cuisine.

Kit Kat
4 Salahadin Street
Jerusalem East
Phone: 284134
Hours: 8–2 and 4–7; closed
Sunday
Dialogue in: English, Arabic,
Hebrew, some German

Pot Luck

No, dear, the subject of this one is not smoking or where to get it. It's back to Mother Earth we go for pots of clay, earthy, primitive planters, spouted water jugs and vases—in all sizes and shapes. Also clay penny-banks and baskets for hanging your jivey ivy and drain pipes to run off the rain.

Find these potties across the alley from the banana man (see "Banana Wherehouse?" page 116) and up under the overhang of Golgotha. Tread lightly because there's a little mosque just opposite where prayers fly 5 times a day and all day Friday. Mohammed will be there on his mountain of pottery. Pleasant and not pushy. Prices are low— hardly haggle-able.

Mohammed Y. Al Dweik Store
Jerusalem East (At the end of the Bus Station where "Bob's Snack Bar" beckons)
Phone: 284081 (neighbor)
Hours: 7–6; closed Friday
Dialogue in: Arabic, English, and a bit of Hebrew

BANANA WHEREHOUSE?

If you're going bananas and don't know where to store them, stop in at what might be the world's only totally underground banana warehouse. It's in the same cave where the Prophet Jeremiah is said to have been stashed because he had the *chutzpah* to babble that the Babylonians were about to do a number on Jerusalem. Old Jer must have been one chilly chap, because this gargantuan grotto (actually an ancient stone quarry), with its 4 unlit fluorescent lights hanging from nowhere, is as cold and as black as can be. A perfect place for cooling it when the heat's on. The bananas are the only bright spot, but seasonal.

Assalam Panais Warehouse
Across from Damascus Gate
Jerusalem East (At the end of the alley to the right of the Bus Station. The alley starts at "Bob's Snack Bar." One cave over from "Pot Luck")
Phone: 284167
Hours: Daytime
Dialogue in: Arabic

Mad for your moniker? You may never see it in lights, but you can say it with flowers: your own name on a hand-painted tile. Hang it on your door or announce your office.

what's on a Name

Marie and Setrak Balian run their 54-year-old workshop, where they design and paint age-old Armenian and Persian designs, fabulous floras and faunas, on mugs, wall or table tiles, pitchers and plates. Get the triple whammy: your name in English, Arabic and Hebrew—or any language your neighbors can or cannot read.

To get the real feel for this pottery, browse around their compound of low-roofed, vine-covered buildings. Sit by the tiled fishpond (no fish). Watch the painters paint and the wheelers at their deal. Name tiles take three weeks or more to emerge, so order early.

Palestinian Pottery
14 Nablus Road (opposite the American Consulate)
Jerusalem East
Phone: 282826
Hours: 9–12:30 and 3–5; closed Sunday
Dialogue in: Armenian, English, French, Hebrew, Arabic and Turkish

117

A California gal gone east, Pat Rainey offers pre-natal exercise and preparation-for-birth classes in her charming home . . . on the right side of the railroad tracks as you travel from town.

Body works and news scoop: ticker tapes

Lessons teach breathing and relaxation exercises plus explanations of how it's done and what to bring to the hospital, and Pat gives that much-needed moral support. Her personal library of hard-to-find books on childbirth, nursing and child-raising is available for on-the-premises reading. Post-natal back-to-shape classes too.

NEWS SCOOP:
TICKER TAPES
Pat has the first small supply of revolutionary "Lullabies from the Womb." These are the recorded sounds from within a future mother's womb (8th month). Pat says: "When played, it immediately soothes and quiets the infant. unless it's sick or wet." Later on in the tape, the sounds of circulating blood and the mother's heart are orchestrated in harmony with suitably classical music.

Pat Rainey
5 Harakevet ("Railroad")
Street, Bak'a
Jerusalem West
Phone: 65133
Dialogue in: English, Hebrew,
and a little Arabic, which she
is now learning so in it she
can also teach

Brick in the Bracken

No matter what the Ministry of Tourism says about sunshine, Jerusalem is clammy cold in winter. Snow, ice, wind, rain, sleet—we get it all. As Christmastime approaches, the mercury may have a place to drop, but what about Santa Claus?

And where to hang your stockings? And where to toast your tootsies? Or marshmallows?

Brickmaster Tuvia Brown can cure your cold: real fireplaces for would-be hotshots.

As you flee our city in search of sun, stop off at the Motza Burnt Tile and Brick Factory. It's the half-century old complex of red-tiled-roof buildings built among the bracken and weeds and flowers and trees just outside town. The red tiles of Jerusalem's oldest picture postcard neighborhoods were all fired at the MBT&BF. They are out of production now, pity, but bricks are still abaking out in them thar hills.

See the monster ovens! See the high brick shoots! See three floors of drying Israeli bricks! See a brick that's beige! See a brick you can see through! See Mr. Brown himself—the only known bachelor in the country!

Motza Burnt Tile and Brick Factory
P.O.B. 6024
Jerusalem Hills
(On the main road to Tel Aviv, turn off at the Motza Inn [on left]. Make a sharp turn left to the road parallel to the highway. Continue to the complex graphically described above)
Phone: 522313
Hours: 7–2; closed Saturday
Dialogue in: German, Hebrew, English, Slavics

Copper Color Tangerine Tone Silverplate Oxidized Baby

who can oxidize your brass, should you want a brownish cast; re-silver your dinnerware; or purge a grubby copper pot, *feenjan* or samovar into a collector's useable.

A select service which no one else in town offers: a lacquer spray to lock in the reincarnated original color.

We had several pieces sprayed five years ago (time marches on), and they are gleaming to this day. Service is fast and dependable, prices are fair. Joseph also has some arty oldies for sale; not great in quantity, but a fun find can occasionally be found.

Nickel-, silver- and gold-plating is Joseph Vander's forte. Plus polishing, and this he does to perfection, on any metal-made treasure you bring him. Twenty years in the same spot, Jerusalem-born Joseph is one of the only crafties

Hamelatesh
17 Salamon Street
Jerusalem West
(Turn right at the bottom
of Shamai Street. His place
is across the street)
Phone: 234376
Hours: 8–1:30 and 2:30–
5:30; Friday till 1:30; closed
Saturday
Dialogue in: Hebrew,
English, Arabic, Yiddish

121

La Dolce Pita

For a big bash, ethnic or otherwise, *pita* (Mideast flat bread) is a must. It accompanies any spread or dip and opens up to accommodate any filling. If you phone ahead (a bit tricky unless your Arabic is good—English they speak, but it's better in person) you can have up to 500 fresh *pitot* (plural) within the hour from Modern Bakery. Or you may prefer to bop in and buy a small bagful.

Fun it is to watch the bakers deftly unloading the oven with their long-handled oar-boards. If you are as amiable as the owner he will roast your eggplants—the place is something of a community kitchen too.

Each *pita* costs 40 agorot, whether you order one or 500; the price does not decrease with an increase in quantity. Real rusks and saffron-colored cakes for sale too.

Sala Hedeq Modern Bakery
21 El-Rashid Street
Jerusalem East (between the Golden Saloon & the Sea Dolphin Restaurant, look for the bright orange door)
Phone: 283548
Hours: Dawn to dark; closed Friday
Dialogue in: Arabic, a little Hebrew, English, Greek

Love Thyself

... in thine own neighborhood. On a secluded, tree-lined street in the German Colony, Jerusalem's own Helena Rubinstein: Grety Varon, a great-looking grandmother who fixes up faces and bods. She dyes eyelashes and/or brows, applies wispy false eyelashes, does pedicures, facials and massages. Two specialties of her house: cold-wax hair removal from legs and special bridal makeups for D-Day. Prices lower than mid-city. Atmosphere relaxed and personal. Appointments best.

Grety Varon
8 Immanuel Noah (off Emek Refaim), German Colony
Jerusalem West
Phone: 34275
Hours: 9–1 and 4–8; closed Friday and Saturday
Dialogue in: Hebrew, Rumanian, German, a little French

what a dreg

You ring the doorbell, Marcelle looks out, then leads you to her kitchen. She brews a cup of Turkish coffee. You drink it, then turn your cup bottoms up. She watches how—for clues to you. She sighs, leans forward over the table, picks up your cup— and tells your destiny in the dregs. Marcelle has been reading for 30 years, says she was born "knowing how." When asked if she can foresee war, Marcelle replied: "War is like gum, you can't get away from it." What a drag.

Marcelle
5 Mordecai Ben Hillel Street
Fourth Floor (above Boutique Balagan)
Downtown Jerusalem West
No Phone
Hours: 1–7; Friday till 3; no Saturdays
Dialogue in: Hebrew, Arabic (bring a bilingual chum)

Pierce de Résistance

The Grafmans, their children, dog, jewelry-making equipment and personal collection of antiques all live in a home built by the Ethiopian Church as pilgrim housing in 1906. The walls are hung with an array of old incense burners, candlesticks and medieval keys. Husband Rafi, renowned for his remarkable repros of 2,000-year-old miniature archaeological items in silver, describes their scene as "an accumulation of the ornamental, occidental and accidental."

Ouch! Sima Grafman got me! Right through the earlobe. She pierces ears right on the spot. Ear-resistible. Especially once you've seen the contents of her cigar boxes: earrings—hand-made, either from scratch or from old jewelry she collects. Delicate and old fashioned. Or fling yourself through Sima's rings. They're ravishing.

Sima & Rafi Grafman
8 Ethiopia Street (you may
miss it once or twice, but it's
there, a great old special
Street)
Jerusalem West
Phone: 223675, for
appointment
Dialogue in: Hebrew, English,
Arabic

Hot pots

From Persia, Russia, North Africa and Bukhara: a top brass and copper collection of antique pots, trays, samovars, gooseneck pitchers, candelabra—all rubbed up to their original soft pinks and golds. David Ezra is well known to Jerusalem copper *cognoscenti* for exquisite antiques. Not an endless array. Go to him for *the* sensational piece. Check carefully the glass-fronted cabinet behind where he sits. That's where he keeps the fancy Persians: densely engraved brass mugs and bowls (the wild old beauties).

Do not expect to bargain. He is super-straight and solidly priced. (The dealers and wheelers come to him.) His father came from Baghdad and opened the shop about 50 years ago, and it enjoys a fine reputation.

If you are specially nice (he has 10 children and one brand-new grandchild—so you know what to talk about) or if you are in the ingroup, Mr. E. may brew a Turkish coffee for you, sweet and sassy. He is a sabra who has never traveled outside Israel but nevertheless speaks all dialects of Arabic, plus Hebrew, Yiddish, English, Kurdistani, Persian and German too.

David Ezra
Merchant of Antiquities
Mea Shearim Market Square
Jerusalem West
(Enter main market square,
first right, third left, next to
Grant Yeshiva Talmud Torah
Free Kitchen)
No phone
Hours: Summer 9–6:30 (no
break); winter 8–5:30;
Friday till 12; closed
Saturday

Voila! Jerusalem's answer to Cartier, Tiffany, and Van Cleef. Nissim Mizrachi, a native son of Persian descent, is a genius jeweler and sculptor. Visit him in his own charming workshop where he will: (1) wow you with good looks and low-key manner, (2) charm you with a cup of Turkish coffee, (3) explain his personal collection of antique pocket watches, decorative mirrors and Moslem metal masks, (4) refuse special orders and (5) not try to sell you anything at all.

His stuff is (1) sensually soft stone-sculpted forms, (2) polished up to satin smooth, (3) farout and fabulous in color (like: verdigris, azure, moss), (4) solid sterling, (5) locked into tiny tears of raw crystal, (6) beyond our descriptive abilities, and (7) beyond most people's pocketbooks.

Nissim Mizrachi
5 Harav David Ben Shimon Street (in the triangle between King David and Agron Streets)
Jerusalem West
Phone: 232970
Hours: As you find him
Dialogue in: Hebrew, English, Arabic, Swedish, German and special Chineese curses

away in a monger | A moveable Beast

Hookers, old and new, from which to hang your sausages or lamps or kitchen utensils or worst enemies. Decorator iron curlicues, gate sections, frames, lamps, and weird old rusty keys (enormous to miniscule). The iron monger himself is a cranky old man who sells his wrought with a touch of wrath. His wares are unusually good. With him, you only need nerves of steel to deal.

Masgeriah ("Ironmongery")
6 Hashikma Street (left off
Mahane Yehuda Road at
18 and downhill), Mahane
Yehuda, Jerusalem West
Hours, phone, languages:
most likely like his neighbors

For Sale: Mules (the star-crossed donkey/horse). An improbable but impregnatable way to carry your cargo or peddle your wares. You make the first low-down offer, and when your price goes up to finally fair, the mule will move to the tune of approximately IL 1,800. The older, the cheaper. Buyer bewarer.

Jericho Road
Jerusalem East
(Past Herod's Gate, turn
sharp right around the wall)
Hours: Fridays between dawn
and 11-ish, or ask around in
the Old City meat market

High Noon with the Nuns

You'll remark enthusiastically after eating ecclesiastically at one of Jerusalem's religious refectory tables. Nuns or brothers provide lunches indigenous to their ilk, which comes in very handy when most everything else is closed on Saturday. To be sure of a place at the parish, phone a day ahead to make your reservation. But if your phone is not working, try your luck and drop in—they will feed you if there's room.

Our sacred selections:

Casa Nova (Franciscan Brothers)
St. Francis Street (not far from the New Gate)
Old City
Phone: 282791
Every day at noon, dinner at 7
Price: IL 15
Dialogue in: Italian, delicate English

Dom Polski (Polish House)
Suq Khan ez-Zeit (Olive Market Street) (Off Aqabat el-Batikh Street, not far from Damascus Gate or the New Gate), Old City
Phone: 282017
Every day at noon
Price: IL 20
Dialogue in: Polish, light English

Les Soeurs de Sion (The Sisters of Zion)
Ein Kerem (village just outside Jerusalem, Bus No. 6/1)
Phone: 415738
Every day at 12:30
Price: IL 25
Dialogue in: French, Hebrew

Ecce Homo—The Sisters of Zion
Via Dolorosa (not far from St. Stephen's Gate, not too far from Damascus Gate)
Old City
Phone: 282445, Sister Donna or Sister Lucy
Every day at 12:30, dinner at 7 too
Price: IL 25
Dialogue in: French, English, Hebrew

There's a pox on lox in the Holy City, but bagels we got. Israeli style: oversized, sesame seeded, crunchy, salty and hot from Mr. Birunfeld's oven. Nightpeople benefit best, since Mr. B. starts baking at 3 a.m. and closes when he wants to, around noonish. For instant energy, or just to look like you belong, buy a bunch of warm ones strung on a string and munch en route to the police station, the Jaffa Gate, Black Panther headquarters, or wherever you're headed. Cheaper than in kiosks, and great for a roll in the day!

Marcus Birunfeld Bakery
9 Kikar Zahal
Jerusalem East-West
(Intersection of Jaffa Road
and Shlomo Hamelech.
Behind our mayor's office
building and near the New Gate)
No Phone
Hours: As above
Dialogue in: Polish, Yiddish,
Russian, Hebrew and a little
German

Snow White

Who knows? The seven dwarfs and a couple of trolls may well be living around where Lydia's studio is at. Hers is a real fairy tale of a neighborhood, stuffed with low-slung stone buildings, red-tiled roofs, arty arches and iron gates.

Lydia makes princess-worthy ceramics and mixes magic into her very own clays and glazes. White on white. Pearly white. White as snow. Translucent white. Sexy delicate white. Slotted spheroids and wafer goblets too. (See them to believe). Each porcelain-clay piece is so light in weight that many, Lydia sadly notes, are lost in the firing. No two are ever alike, although all are distinctively high her-style.

In Poland, Lydia earned an M.A. in Law and started ceramics about 10 years ago when she arrived in Israel. She is already on her way to international renown.

So catch her while you can. Call and meet in her artful home and walk together to her studio, where she keeps the wheels, kiln, other accoutrements and many pretty porcelains. It's a 2-minute walk to the little street with the big name: Zariel Hildesheimer?!

Lydia Zavadsky
1 Hamagid Street
(off Emek Refaim)
German Colony
Jerusalem West
Phone: 60087, evenings, for
appointment
Dialogue in: Polish, Hebrew,
English, Russian

Kaballah in Katamon

This one is so far out, we can only tell it like it was. Ask anyone in Katamon-Hay how to find Abu Daoud, and it works— you'll find him, the locally renowned rabbi who reads fortunes, makes blessings, sees past, present, and future, and offers counsel on the basis of a secret The entrance to his small cottage augers mid-east and mid-earth. Outside, a black cat stares from atop a heap of old open jars, springs from something, used sponges and croaking cacti. Inside is a cabal of kabbalists, friends, family, supplicants, mendicants, the worried, the happy, et al. The scene is a kaleidoscope of recyclables: old newspapers, jars half-filled with stuff, scissor parts, flea-market-style furniture. Rabbi Abu Daoud Shohet, Iraqi born, remarks on your fortune by reading from the *Goral Hakadosh* (literally, "The Fate of the Holy"). With us, Abu D. warmed up and became paternal and personal, blessing our frazzled brains and bent minds. Since we didn't ask for advice, we didn't get any, but that's what he offers to the regulars who come to see him. He has, in fact, a coterie of loyal constants. Definitely not for everyone. text.

Rabbi Abu Daoud Shohet
16 Barniki Street, Katamon-Hay, Jerusalem West
(On Yohanan Ben Zakkai, take your last right [no pun] before the right turn leading to the Delek Gas Station. Across from No. 11 Barniki, up the steps, first gate on left)
Phone: 62239, which he may or may not answer
Hours: 8–5; no Fridays or Saturdays
Dialogue in: Hebrew with Arabic accent, Persian, Turkish

the end...?

It's the wind-up of the Wonderground. Wondering what's next? Find out in the triumphant sequel to this book, due the twelfth of never. Meanwhile, rest and relax at The Little Gallery.

A glass of wine, a lot of art, and chow beside you. Plus good company, classical music, Gaza-material pillows and sweet Yossi Ofek, host of this art gallery with all the comforts. He puts up a different show every three weeks, often the first exhibition of a young Israeli artist's work. The Gallery's latest cook is a new immigrant from Russia—catch his kneidlach while you watch the local talent, both hanging on the walls and hanging around this very in and very charming place. Come mid-morning for spiced tea, mid-day for a cheese board or at midnight for everything.

The Little Gallery
Proprietor, Yossi Ofek
27 Salamon Street
Nahlat Sheva
Downtown Jerusalem West
Phone: 233631
Hours: 10 a.m.–2 p.m.; 6 p.m.–1 a.m.; Friday till 3 p.m.; open at 6 p.m. on Saturday
Dialogue in: Almost any language

The Underground Guides

Judy Stacey Goldman & *Janet Kaplan*

JERUSALEM ARRIVALS

May 6, 1968
via El Al
to Lod Airport
Baggage

July 12, 1968
via S.S. Adria
to Haifa Port
No baggage

The last word

"NEW YORK
HAS EVERYTHING
EXCEPT JERUSALEM"

Joan Silberstein
Holyland Hosteler
Word Watcher and
Wonderwoman of the
Workshop Off Main Street

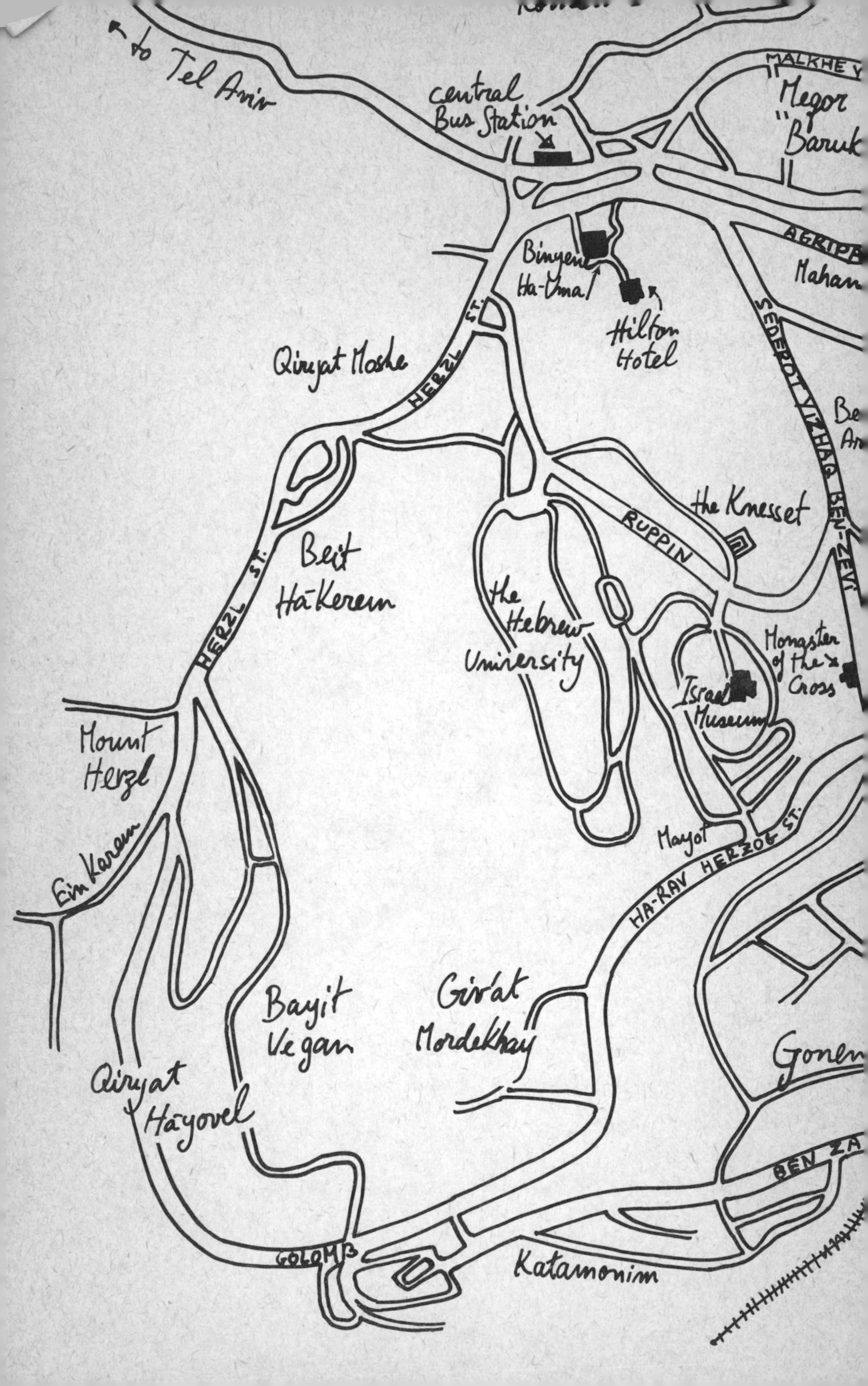

to Tel Aviv
Central Bus Station
MALKHE Y
Meqor Baruk
AGRIPP
Mahan
Binyene Ha-Uma
Hilton Hotel
SEDEROT YIZHAQ BEN-ZEVI
Qiryat Moshe
HERZL ST.
Be Am
the Knesset
RUPPIN
Beit Ha-Kerem
the Hebrew University
Monaster of the Cross
Israel Museum
Mount Herzl
Ein Karem
Mayot
HA-RAV HERZOG ST.
Bayit Vegan
Giv'at Mordekhay
Gonen
Qiryat Ha-yovel
BEN ZA
GOLOMB
Katamonim

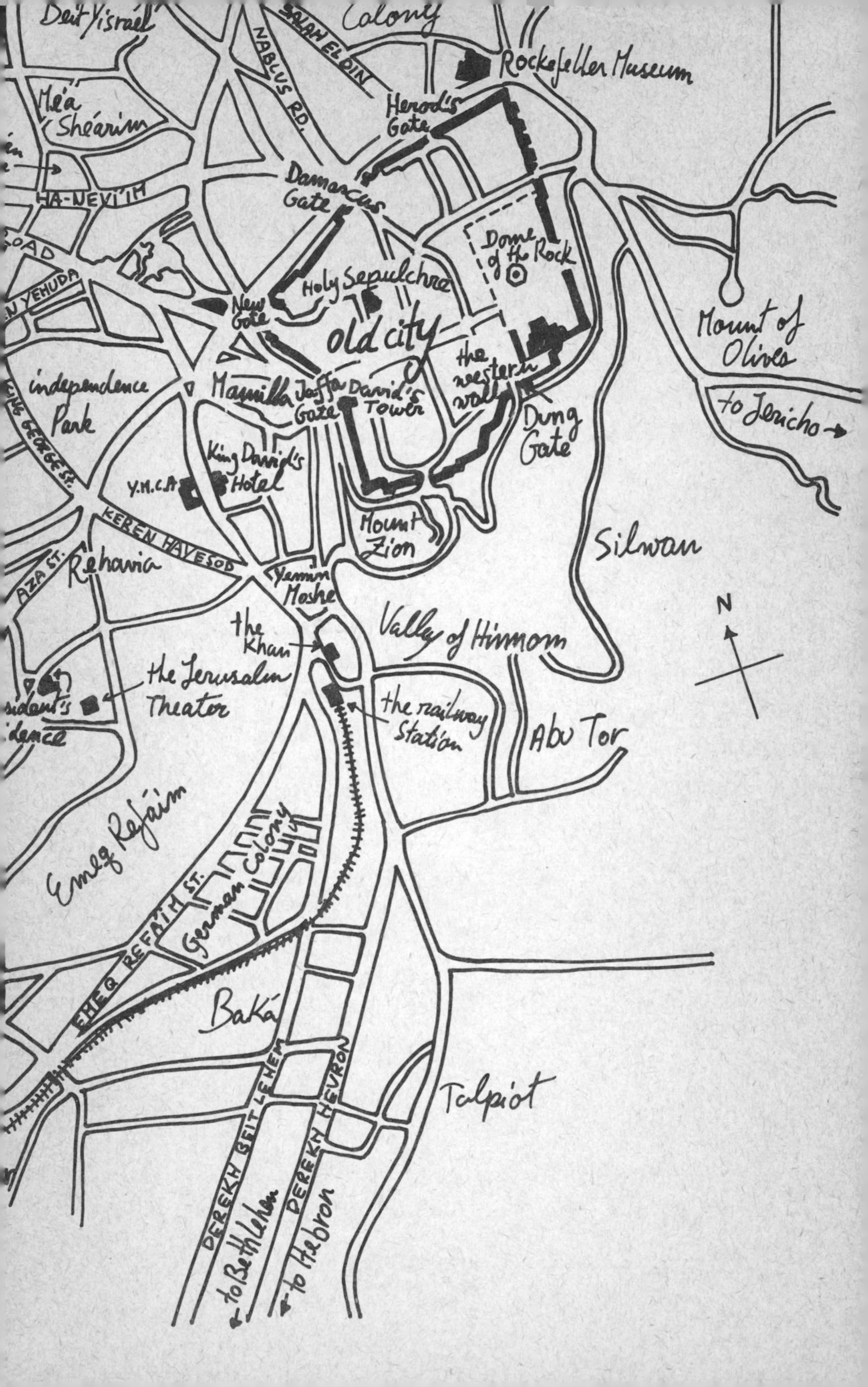
Beit Yisráel
Colony
SALAH EL DIN
NABLUS RD.
Rockefeller Museum
Méa Shéarim
Herod's Gate
HA-NEVI'IM
Damascus Gate
Dome of the Rock
Holy Sepulchre
New Gate
old city
Mount of Olives
the western wall
independence Park
Mamilla
Jaffa Gate
David's Tower
Dung Gate
to Jericho
KING GEORGE ST.
King David's Hotel
Y.M.C.A.
KEREN HAYESOD
Mount Zion
Silwan
Rehavia
AZA ST.
Yemin Moshe
the Khan
Valley of Hinnom
N
the Jerusalem Theater
the railway Station
Abu Tor
Emeq Refaim
German Colony
EMEQ REFAIM ST.
Baká
Talpiot
DEREKH BEIT LEHEM
DEREKH HEVRON
to Bethlehem
to Hebron

INDEX